"Many consumers who have had their identity stolen find themselves in a seemingly endless Kafkaesque nightmare of relentless bill collectors and indifferent law enforcement agencies more concerned with other priorities. Their pleas are ignored by credit card companies who are only interested in collecting money and they are further victimized by credit bureaus who pay lip service to their obligations under the Fair Credit Reporting Act. Safeguard Your Identity *is a potent ally that empowers consumers, enables them to marshal their resources, fight back and regain their identity."*

—James B. Fishman, Consumer Attorney, New York, NY

"Safeguard Your Identity *is a timely and user-friendly guide to protecting your good name in the Electronic Age. Highly recommended to anyone who wants to avoid being the next victim of America's fastest-growing form of white collar crime."*

—Thomas A. Papageorge, criminal attorney, consumer fraud prosecutor, legislative advocate, Los Angeles, CA

"Identity Theft is growing rapidly and catching consumers blindly. Oftentimes, you never know you are the victim of this crime until the damage is done. Reading Mari Frank's book, Safeguard Your Identity, *is the first and most important step you can take to protect yourself before this happens to you. This book should be a household item."*

—Larry Smith, consumer rights attorney, Chicago, IL

"If you're at all concerned about identity theft—and you should be if you have anything to lose and your time and reputation is valuable to you—you must read Safeguard Your Identity. *And, more importantly, you need to do what Mari outlines to protect you and your family from this growing new threat to our peace of mind and financial security."*

—Greg Sherwood, Television Host,
KQED Public Television, San Francisco, CA

"As an identity theft prosecutor, lecturer, ***and victim,*** *I have been helping the public stop this fraud scourge for years; but I have never seen a single resource for victim protection and remedies with as much thoroughness and helpful detail as Mari Frank's* Safeguard Your Identity. *Not just a 'must-read' but a 'must-act-upon' book for all victims and soon-to-be victims."*

—Jerry Coleman, criminal attorney, prosecutor,
San Francisco, CA

"Before identity theft was recognized as a specific crime that could be prosecuted, Mari Frank was on the cutting edge of educating citizens and lawmakers about the building threat of identity theft. Her book Safeguard Your Identity *is a must read for everyone. Whether you are coping with being the victim of identity theft, looking for steps to protect your financial integrity, or working in a business entrusted with customers' personal information—Mari's book offers critical advice."*

—Greg Brose, criminal attorney, prosecutor, Ventura , CA

"Your credit history affects more than just your ability to get a loan—it touches many aspects of your life, from getting a job to obtaining insurance to affecting the rates your existing creditors charge you. Safeguard Your Identity *is the premier source of the best means available to protect your identity and your all important credit history from the ever-increasing threat of Identity Theft."*

—Chris E. Kittell, Esq., consumer lawyer,
Webster, Gresham, and Kittell, Clarksdale, MS

"I found Safeguard Your Identity *not only informative, but very practical—especially the 20 steps to take once fraud is discovered. I will give this book to my daughter, who doesn't believe my wife and me when we tell her to shred her pre-approved credit card mailings etc. She feels that Identity Theft is something that happens to someone else! Also, this book should be displayed in the lobbies of banks, credit unions, and other financial institutions, so that the public can become better educated about this epidemic!"*

—Norman K. K. Lau, consumer lawyer, Honolulu, HI

"I found Mari Frank's book Safeguard Your Identity *a GREAT resource for the prevention of Identity Theft. But for those unfortunate individuals who are the victim of Identity Theft, this book is also a valuable tool in their quest to correct their good name. The book provides numerous tips and web sites that can help an Identity Theft victim right the wrong."*

—Clayton S. Morrow, consumer attorney, Pittsburgh, PA

SAFEGUARD YOUR IDENTITY:

Protect Yourself With A Personal Privacy Audit

Mari J. Frank, Esq.

PORPOISE PRESS, INC.

Safeguard Your Identity:
Protect Yourself With a Personal Privacy Audit

Library of Congress Cataloging-in-Publication Data

Frank, Mari J.
Safeguard your identity : protect yourself with a personal privacy audit / Mari J. Frank. -- 1st ed. -- Laguna Niguel, CA : Porpoise Press, 2005.
p. ; cm.
ISBN: 1-892126-06-0
1. Identity theft--United States--Prevention. 2. Imposters and imposture--United States. 3. False personation--United States. 4. Consumer protection--United States. 5. Victims of crimes--Handbooks, manuals, etc. I. Title.

HV6759 .F736 2005 2004097399
364.16/3--dc22 0410

Printed in the U.S.A.: First Printing 2005

9 8 7 6 5 4 3

SAFEGUARD YOUR IDENTITY:

Protect Yourself With A Personal Privacy Audit

By Mari J. Frank, Esq.

PORPOISE PRESS, INC.
28202 Cabot Road, Suite 300
Laguna Niguel, CA 92677 U.S.A.
To order this title and other publications,
please call (800) 725-0807

web site: Identity Theft Prevention and Survival
www.identitytheft.org

FOREWORD

If you have this book in hand, you are probably concerned about Safeguarding Your Identity—and you should be! In 1997, I became a victim of identity theft when my employer stole my identity. Back then, there was little information about identity theft victimization; in fact, few people even knew what I was talking about.

Thankfully, Mari Frank did. As a former victim herself, and self-taught expert on this crime, she spent time advising me through the process. I don't know what I would have done without her support over the years. As a result of my experience, and with Mari's encouragement, my husband and I founded the nonprofit Identity Theft Resource Center (ITRC). Along with Ms. Frank, and other consumer groups, we serve thousands of victims throughout our country. We have been honored to sit beside Mari on committees, in legislative hearings and on task forces that have changed laws. Jointly, we have promoted more sensitivity toward victims, more accountability in the financial industry, better understanding from law enforcement, and positive communication among the various groups that need to work collaboratively.

No one can promise you that you can absolutely prevent identity theft, but this book will help you understand this crime, and help you greatly minimize your risk. We all need to attack identity theft on many levels. We must become keenly aware of the manner in which information is stolen, how it is used, and ways to reduce risk. This book will show you how to defend yourself as an individual, employee, consumer, and a business manager or owner.

As you read through this book, you'll see that much of the advice will affect you at home as well as in commerce. The true battle will be fought in the business world, since corporate America is the main repository for much of our personal information. For example, you will read that it is vital to shred paper documents with identifying information and not just to put them in a dumpster or the trash. It is clear that consumers and businesses alike should embrace this practice.

At first glance, you'll look at this personal privacy audit and think you need to make many lifestyle changes. However, when you consider the consequences, and take just a few pages at a time, you will probably find it easy to accomplish these changes with minimal effort.

Identity theft is a fact in this information age. We cannot escape that it is an epidemic. We cannot bury our heads in the sand like ostriches. However, we also don't have to be trapped by our fear of this crime. Once you read this book, you will understand this crime, and how to incorporate protection measures into your daily life. You'll even learn the steps to take if you fall victim. You will also realize that even if you become a victim, it is not a death sentence. This book, and Mari's other newly revised book, *From Victim to Victor: A Step By Step Guide to Ending the Nightmare of Identity Theft* will help you guard yourself, and give you the tools you need to get your life back if you become a victim of this crime.

Safeguard Your Identity: Protect Yourself with a Personal Privacy Audit is a book that should not sit on a shelf. I recommend you place it where you will read it page by page and apply and incorporate the suggestions. We guarantee that with each reading you will find one more tip or piece of information you haven't thought about and that you need to implement for your privacy protection plan.

The Identity Theft Resource Center would not exist without the groundwork and support of people like Mari Frank. We consider her our friend, and we are proud to have her wise counsel as a member of our advisory board. Because of her expertise as an attorney, professional trainer, and sheriff reserve, we cannot think of a better person to write this book. Mari will effectively guide you on your journey through the world of safeguarding your identity.

Linda Foley
Executive Director
The Identity Theft Resource Center, San Diego, CA
www.idtheftcenter.org

Acknowledgements

This book could not have materialized without the extraordinary efforts and assistance of many fabulous and dedicated people. I feel so honored and blessed to be able to thank them in this book and send them all of my gratitude and love for their support.

To Linda Foley, the co-executive director of the Identity Theft Resource Center, who wrote the foreword to this book. I am so thankful to her and her husband Jay, who co-founded the Center. They have been a wonderful help to so many victims of identity theft. The work that they've done through the years, with enthusiasm, dedication, and tenacity, has been a godsend to so many victims. I'm honored to be Linda and Jay's friend, colleague, and privileged member of the Identity Theft Resource Center's Advisory Board.

To Beth Givens, the director of the Privacy Rights Clearinghouse, who was the original pioneer that led the way for all of us who have joined her journey to help thousands of identity theft victims. Beth has been a mentor, supporter, and friend to me through the years. She also helped Linda Foley (Linda and I were both former victims of this crime) create the Identity Theft Resource Center. Beth urged Linda and me to help others, just as she has provided tremendous assistance to victims herself. She encouraged me to write my book *From Victim to Victor: A Step by Step Guide To Ending the Nightmare of Identity Theft* and to develop and write

The Identity Theft Survival Kit. Beth and I enjoyed co-authoring the booklet *Privacy Piracy: A Guide To Protecting Yourself From Identity Theft,* which served as a predecessor to this book. I am grateful to Beth for sharing her knowledge and expertise with me. The Privacy Rights Clearinghouse has been instrumental in providing testimony, publications, and fact sheets to enhance and defend privacy in our society.

To Anthony Tiano, CEO of Santa Fe Productions. He's been a guru and motivating force in the creation of this book. I'm humbled and privileged that he gave me the exciting opportunity to share my privacy and identity theft concerns, research, and expertise with the PBS television audience. Tony enlisted me to host and present the television seminar "Identity Theft: Protecting Yourself in the Information Age." His request that I update my writings to help the viewing audience protect their identity, was the impetus for *Safeguard Your Identity: Protect Yourself With A Personal Privacy Audit*. His belief in the public's need for this book prompted him to enlist me to develop several educational items for a PBS television pledge drive that began in late 2004. This book, and my book *From Victim to Victor: A Step-by-Step Guide to Ending the Nightmare of Identity Theft* (Second Edition, with the CD of legal letters, logs, and resources) were the pledge gifts that audience members received when they contributed donations to support public television. Tony has been an inspiring sage, and has taught me a great deal about how ethical producers create great learning opportunities. I'm appreciative of his professionalism and continual optimism.

To my new friend and enthusiastic assistant, Lori Rodriguez, who jumped in with both feet to help transcribe my dictation and decipher my hieroglyphics. She came to my office on a strange coincidence, and I know that she was sent to me from above as a helping angel in disguise.

To Ellen Felton, my excellent long-time administrative assistant and dear friend, who has been my chief supporter, cheerleader, confidant, and kindred spirit for many years. She has helped console hundreds of concerned consumers and distraught victims herself, and has continued to have patience and perseverance through our many diverse projects.

To my terrific children, Bryan and Alyssa, hopefully my privacy and identity theft efforts will make the world a safer place for their future and their own children's future.

To Vicki Gibbs, my amazing editor, who exchanged e-mails and files with me across the miles to support me and keep the process going in a timely manner. Her literary skills, organizational talents, and affirmative attitude made my hectic schedule a much more positive experience.

To Cynthia Frank, my inspiring project coordinator, and her team of publishing experts. I am grateful to her and her team for their excellent suggestions, warmth, help, and guidance in this project. Although she is no relation to me, she treated me like family with her kind assistance.

To my fabulous husband, Lloyd Boshaw, Jr., my soul mate, and greatest friend. I appreciate his support, love, and astonishing sense of humor . . . not to mention his patience—especially on those nights that he would wait good-naturedly while I burned the midnight oil. I thank him for all the delicious dinners and healthy breakfasts he cooked for me so that I could focus on my writing. I'm truly blessed by having this caring man in my life.

To my adorable golden retriever, Raido, who kept my feet warm while I spent hours at the computer. He knew when to nudge my arm with his cold nose, pushing my hand off the keyboard, insisting I take a walking-break. His loyalty, quiet companionship, and never-ending tail wagging kept me upbeat even when I felt stressed.

To my dear sister and best friend, Anita. Although she was taken from us suddenly last year, I still feel her presence and love. I greatly miss her nurturing support, but I'm grateful for the time we shared.

To the numerous privacy, financial, and law enforcement experts, who graciously enlightened me with their insights, I am appreciative.

And to the many remarkable victims of identity theft who generously shared their stories, concerns, and hearts with me, thank you.

Most importantly, I express my gratitude to God for the guidance, inspiration, and love I receive each day.

Mari Frank

Contents

Introduction:

Assess What You Already Know

Are You Safeguarding Your Identity?

You probably think that identity theft could never happen to you. You might be surprised. Before you begin to take stock of your susceptibility to losing your identity, try this simple True/False test to see how much you already know about how to protect yourself from this sinister crime. You'll find the answers and explanations on the pages following the quiz. Don't worry about your score; this exercise is your private evaluation, to show you why you need to read the rest of this book.

TRUE or FALSE?

1. If you don't use a computer, or if you do but you never use the Internet, you don't have to worry about becoming a victim of identity theft.
   ❑ **true** ❑ **false**

2. If your credit cards always stay safely in your wallet, you don't have to worry about someone abusing them.
   ❑ **true** ❑ **false**

3. The most important method to shield yourself from becoming a victim of financial identity theft is to order your credit reports at least twice a year from the three major credit reporting agencies: Equifax, Experian, TransUnion.
   ❑ **true** ❑ **false**

4. It's safer to use a credit card than your personal check.
   ❑ **true** ❑ **false**

5. Your transactions are more secure when you use an ATM debit card with a Visa/MasterCard logo than if you use a regular credit card.
   ❑ **true** ❑ **false**

6. Someone can steal your identity without using your name.
   ❑ **true** ❑ **false**

7. Using your mother's maiden name as your password will prevent you from becoming a victim of fraud.
   ❑ **true** ❑ **false**

8. If you have a healthcare card like a Medicare/Medicaid card or insurance card that has your Social Security number on it, you must carry it in your wallet at all times, with your number fully displayed in case you are in an accident.
   ❑ **true** ❑ **false**

9. When receiving an authentic-looking e-mail from your bank, financial institution, the IRS, the FDIC, etc. asking you for personal information including your Social Security number, credit card numbers, or other personal information, you should NEVER respond at all to that e-mail.
   ❑ **true** ❑ **false**

10. If you learn that someone has used your identity in another state, the first thing to do is call that state's attorney general.
❑ **true** ❑ **false**

11. When using your cell phone or your remote, wireless (portable) home phone, you should feel secure giving your credit card information over the phone to order products or services.
❑ **true** ❑ **false**

12. The best way to deal with pre-approved offers and other junk mail that you receive is to immediately dump it in the garbage, or mark it "refused" or "return to sender" and place it in a mailbox.
❑ **true** ❑ **false**

13. If you're looking for a job, it's important to expose yourself to as many employers as possible by posting your job application, résumé, work history, and important personal background information on the Internet.
❑ **true** ❑ **false**

14. When using your wireless laptop at the airport or at Starbuck's, you are exposing your personal information to "drive-by hackers."
❑ **true** ❑ **false**

15. No one is immune to identity theft.
❑ **true** ❑ **false**

These Answers May Astound You

1. **If you don't use a computer, or if you do but you never use the Internet, you don't have to worry about becoming a victim of identity theft.**

   False—Most identity thieves actually steal your personal information off-line. They do this in a variety of ways, possibly by dumpster diving in your own garbage. (By the way, your garbage does not belong to you once you put it on the curb. Anyone is free to take it without breaking the law. Obviously, if they use it to commit fraud they are violating the law.) They also can get your personal information, including your Social Security number, from many places. For example, your personal and confidential data is available at: your doctor's office, your accountant's office, various government agencies (such as the Social Security Administration and the IRS,) your employer's personnel office, your mortgage lender, your bank, etc. Your personal information is collected and bought, and then sold and maintained in many databases across the country. You have no idea how many companies store your information, who has access to it, or how it is being transferred, shared, or marketed. So, whether or not you use a computer or are totally a "non-techie," doesn't matter. No one is exempt from identity theft. There are many things you can do to protect yourself in your home, at work, and while shopping that have nothing to do with the Internet. When you read the next three chapters, you'll find out much more about how to protect your identity in the real world as well as in the virtual world of the Internet.

2. **If your credit cards always stay safely in your wallet, you don't have to worry about someone abusing them.**

   False—Anyone can use your credit card number and expiration date online or on the phone to purchase goods and services without having the card in hand. The good news is federal law protects you from fraud. If any fraudulent charges appear on your credit card, and you notify the bank immediately upon receiving your billing statement, the most you will be liable for is the first $50, and most companies will even waive any costs. Therefore, it's critical that you check all of your credit card statements and make sure that you recognize every charge listed. If you discover a credit charge that you don't recognize, call the 800 number listed on your statement and confirm with the vendor that it was a legitimate charge. Often when you buy products over the phone or online, the merchant account name is different than the actual product name that you purchased, so it may look unfamiliar. Check it out first (to refresh your memory of a purchase you may have made). If it is a scam, immediately call your credit card company and notify them, cancel the account, and get yourself a replacement credit card with a new number. (You will have to reestablish any auto-pay accounts.) Change your mother's maiden name or former password to a new password and flag the account for fraud.

3. **The most important method to shield yourself from becoming a victim of financial identity theft is to order your credit reports at least twice a year from the three major credit reporting agencies: Equifax, Experian, TransUnion.**
True—Financial identity theft will show up immediately on your credit profile. Credit reports are not always easy to read, especially since the three major companies have different formats. However, consider frequent reviews of your profile an investment in protecting yourself. We suggest that you get your credit reports at least twice a year. Under federal law, you are entitled to get one free credit report per year from each of

the credit reporting agencies. We suggest that you do so, since they are competitors and you may find fraud on one report and not on the others. It's important to go over these credit reports with a fine-tooth comb. We'll tell you how to read your credit reports in Chapter Six, and we'll tell you about options such as credit monitoring companies.

4. **It's safer to use a credit card than your personal check.**
True—Using a personal check can expose you to fraud that is harder to remedy than fraud from a credit card. Your check has the account and routing numbers printed at the bottom. Many people will even put their whole name, address, driver's license number, and without thinking, print their Social Security number on their checks as well. All this information, along with your check, is all that a fraudster needs to steal all the money from your account. If you use your credit card instead of a check, you'll have the chance to stop any fraud before the bill is paid. If you're not able to pay by credit card, another alternative is to use pay-by-phone, which you initiate from your bank. Each month you key in your payment using your phone. You pay bills you wish, and your bank then directly disburses electronically or by draft to the payee. Then, if the recipient says he has not been paid, your bank deals with the problem, not you. It reduces the chance of theft. (By the way, pay your bills using a "landline," not a wireless remote; we will tell you why later.)

Online banking is another option. Although the banks tout this as a very secure way to pay your bills, because of online vulnerabilities and the sensitivity of the information you are placing on your computer, we suggest that presently it is a safer bet to pay bills by phone (landline) than through the Internet. But online banking is probably more secure than using a hard copy check! For businesspersons, we acknowledge that using a check to pay bills is still quite the norm. We encourage you to use a credit card whenever possible.

Other reasons not to use personal checks: If you put your bill payments in an envelope, in your mailbox, with the little, red flag raised, you make life easy for fraudsters passing by the neighborhood looking for your paid bills. These adept thieves can easily steal your mail, acid wash the names of the recipients on the checks, write in their own names, and then cash your checks, with your own valid signature.

Nowadays, office supply stores provide blank computer checks for you to imprint your bank account and routing number to personalize your checks. A savvy imposter can take your routing number and copy information from your check, prepare and cash new checks, and drain your account of funds. Additionally, perpetrators deposit other fraudulent checks into your account, and soon after, write checks from your account for goods and service. Not only is the bank defrauded, but you are also swindled. Although the banks say that you are protected and will be reimbursed, victims experience delays, bounced checks, embarrassment, and frustration. You're actually safer using a credit card so you can monitor and review your credit card statements each month prior to paying. You only pay those bills that are truly yours.

5. **Your transactions are more secure when you use an ATM debit card with a Visa / MasterCard logo than if you use a regular credit card.**

   False!—If you use a debit card with the Visa or MasterCard logo on it to pay for goods, your money is removed immediately from your checking account, before you have a chance to even review the charges. With a normal credit card, you charge the products and services, and at the end of the month you review the billing statement before you pay the bill. You have a chance to ascertain if there is any fraud first, and you don't have to worry about money being depleted from your account without your knowledge.

We've had many clients call saying that the number from their debit Visa / MasterCard was used (without the card) by phone or on the Internet. Unbeknownst to them, money was removed from the account, causing checks written by the victim to bounce. This not only created problems with the victim's own creditors—causing late payments, resulting in late fees, and ruining that person's financial reputation—but it also ended up costing these victims their check-cashing privileges due to insufficient funds. So, you are much safer using a credit card than your debit card for purchases.

Some parents give their child a checking account with an ATM debit card that has a Visa / MasterCard logo. They consider this a good way to limit their children (often college students) to charging only the amount in the account. But, since many college students become victims of fraud, we suggest instead, providing them with a credit card that has a minimum amount of credit available. This will also help young people learn not to overspend. Also, prepaid credit cards are available; a set amount is paid on the card prior to its issue. In today's easy credit society, we have many alternatives to ensure that we don't spend beyond our means, so consider the consequences when making your choice.

Note that your bank will automatically send you your ATM / debit card with the Visa / MasterCard logo when you open a checking account. Those cards are great moneymakers for financial institutions. You can call your bank and ask them to issue you a new card without any Visa / MasterCard logo. (Don't forget to cancel the previously sent card.) You can still use your simple ATM card to get cash or deposit funds anywhere in the world at any ATM Machine. By the way, we suggest you use only use ATM machines located at banks or credit unions (well lit, safe areas), since anyone can purchase an ATM machine and set it up as a scam to skim your information and capture your password.

6. **Someone can steal your identity without using your name.**
   True—We've had people call to inform us that their identity was stolen using their Social Security number with an entirely different name. In fact, some victims learn their impostor is even a different gender and race. We've had women whose identities were stolen by men, even using masculine names. The Social Security number is the "key to the kingdom" for financial fraud and for criminal identity theft. The Social Security number can be used with the wrong name and date of birth. That's why it's so important that you guard your Social Security number and other personal identifiers. There are ways to do this that we will tell you about in Chapters Two and Three. Unfortunately, you don't have control over the many ways in which your Social Security number is shared and sold. In later chapters, we will talk about some barriers you can erect to minimize your risk of losing your identity.

7. **Using your mother's maiden name as your password will prevent you from becoming a victim of fraud.**
   False—Your mother's maiden name, which many banks ask for as your "password," is readily available to thieves because it is written on your birth certificate, a public record, which also may appear on the Internet. Some states, like California,

are trying to eliminate the amount of personal information that is divulged on birth and death certificates; but most states do not yet have laws to protect that information. Therefore, we strongly suggest that you instruct those banks and financial institutions that urge you to use your mother's maiden name as your personal password, to allow you to change the password to a unique word (not your pets' names, not your children's names, but a unique name mixed with numbers.) So, change your mother's maiden name on all of your accounts to your unique secret password . . . and don't tell others this word. When opening a new account, you may find that many businesses still have a space on their application for your mother's maiden name—just use a password instead.

8. **If you have a healthcare card like a Medicare / Medicaid card or insurance card that has your Social Security number on it, you must carry it in your wallet at all times, with your Social Security number fully displayed in case you are in an accident.**

   False–If your wallet is lost or stolen, the cards with your Social Security number on them can be used to steal your identity. Take those cards that have your Social Security number on them out of your wallet. Make a duplicate copy of the cards, then black out all but the last four numbers on each card and place the copy back in your wallet. Make sure that only the last four numbers are visible. If you're in an accident or you have need to use the hospital services or services of some other agency, authorities will be able to match the information on the card with the last four numbers and find you in their databases to provide you the services you need. It's a good idea for you to memorize your Social Security number, and keep the actual card in a locked cabinet in your home.

9. **When receiving an authentic-looking e-mail from your bank, financial institution, the IRS, the FDIC, etc. asking you for personal information including your Social Security number, credit card numbers, or other personal information, you should NEVER respond at all to that e-mail.**
   True—If you worry that the authentic, official-looking e-mail may be true, your best action is to call the number of the credit card company or the agency that you find listed on a previous billing statement to make sure that the request is legitimate. (Never call the number listed in the e-mail, because it could be fraudulent. Never "get hooked" into responding to the "phishing expedition." You may have received e-mails from Nigeria telling you that the sender is a princess who has come into money and that if you provide her with some funds to secure the account, then she will share her inheritance with you. Don't ever believe these scams. Anything that seems too good to be true is "too good to be true." If you respond to any of these "phishing" e-mails, then the perpetrators will have your e-mail address and perhaps even your name showing on your reply. Then they may further contact you. So, it's best to either delete these or forward them to the FBI or the Federal Trade Commission. You may forward this type of spam to spam@uce.gov. Also see the resource list in Chapter Eight.)

10. **If you learn that someone has used your identity in another state, the first thing to do is call that state's attorney general.**
   False—If you find out that someone is using your identity in another state or another county, the first thing you should do is call the credit reporting agencies and place a fraud alert on your credit profile. (See Chapter Six to learn How to Regain Your Financial Health and Good Name.) When you contact law

enforcement (city police or county sheriff), call your local police or sheriff in the city or the county in which you live. You must get a police report, and it's highly unlikely that law enforcement in another jurisdiction will take the report because they will be worried that if they do, they'll need to investigate. It will be very challenging for them to investigate when the victim resides in another state. Resources are limited, and they are overwhelmed by too many victims in their own area. Therefore, report the fraud in your local law enforcement jurisdiction, and ask them to contact the police agency where the fraud is taking place. If you visit **www.consumer.gov/idtheft** you can click on the laws of your state, as well as the laws of the state in which the perpetrator is using your name. Print a copy of the penal code sections from your state and call the police to report the particular type of fraud per the penal code section. Your local police agency may be willing to help you (they must make at least an informational report) and willing to investigate (although oftentimes they don't have enough money or investigators to do so). They may be willing to call the FBI or the Secret Service, who also have jurisdiction over federal financial crimes if the case is appropriate, or, for example, if the crime crosses state lines. Additionally, your local law enforcement may stand a better chance of motivating the law enforcement agency in the state where the crime was committed. The most important task for victims is to get an informational police report so they can comply with requirements to regain their identities.

11. **When using your cell phone or your remote, wireless (portable) home phone, you should feel secure giving your credit card information over the phone to order products or services.**

False—Only provide sensitive or confidential information, including credit card numbers, when using a landline. Wireless devices such as your cell phone and remote wireless phones in your house are not secure from the scamming devices of hackers. There are numerous technology tools that allow criminal ears to listen in on wireless telephone conversations.

12. **The best way to deal with pre-approved offers and other junk mail that you receive is to immediately dump it in the garbage, or mark it "refused" or "return to sender" and place it in a mailbox.**
False—Your best alternative for stopping those pre-approved offers is to call the opt-out number: 1-888-5-OPT-OUT. The credit reporting agencies combine your financial profile in a database with other people of like financial status and lifestyle. Your name and profile are sold on promotion with thousands of other names to the credit card companies who wish to purchase that database. Then, pre-approved offers are sent to you in the mail for you to respond with an acceptance. Rather than tossing these in the trash (giving fraudsters an opportunity to dumpster dive and obtain the applications to reply to the offers and steal your identity), or sending them back in the mail (which may enable fraudsters to steal that mail), opt out of having your name sold on promotion with the credit reporting agencies; then shred the offers before discarding.

Additionally, you can write to your credit card companies and financial institutions that you wish to opt out of having your information shared and sold by them too. When you receive the financial privacy notices in the mail from your banks and credit card companies, don't just toss them in the trash. Take the opportunity to opt out of allowing those companies to sell your information. In most states, and federally, your information is bought, sold, and shared without your prior permission. Under federal law, financial institutions can sell or share your personal information unless you opt out. Fortunately, some states are beginning to be more privacy-conscious. California and North Dakota passed laws that require companies to get your permission prior to selling your information. This method of stopping the sharing of your information is called "opt-in." You have more control over the sharing of that information when you opt-in. I encourage you to ask your state legislators to pass laws requiring "opt-in" (where you consent if you wish) procedures for the sale of your private data.

I'm hopeful that because some states are taking privacy more seriously, that reputable companies will step up to the plate and offer all Americans the opportunity to give prior permission to allow the sale of their information. That's not the case right now, however, so you still have the burden of stopping companies from selling your information, and you can see more about how to do that in Chapter Two.

13. **If you're looking for a job, it's important to expose yourself to as many employers as possible by posting your job application, résumé, work history, and important personal background information on the Internet.**

False—With the information that you provide online for employment purposes, someone can steal your identity and obtain a job using your résumé and background. Not only can this thief become employed using your good name, (and then of course you are liable for all the taxes,) but they can also do worse things, such as commit crimes or terrorist acts. We suggest that you apply directly to the company that is interested in you as a candidate, and give your personal information only when you are directly interacting with a known company.

Never put your Social Security number online. In fact, until you are seriously considered for hiring, you need not supply your Social Security number or other sensitive facts.

14. **When using your wireless laptop at the airport or at Starbuck's, you are exposing your personal information to "drive-by hackers."**
   True—Although wi-fi (wireless) networks are tremendously popular, since you can communicate online, and surf the Web in public meeting places, or have Internet access all through your house without burdensome network cables, you are exposing yourself to danger. Wi-fi radio signals broadcast long distances. If you have unsecured wireless, not only do you expose yourself to an attack through your bandwidth, but also "drive-by or walk-by hackers" can get into your system and raid your files. If you have any sensitive information, including your credit card numbers and personal identifiers on your laptop or home computer, you risk losing your identity to theft. This book will show you steps to protect yourself. But the safest way to avoid data theft is to not keep sensitive personal information about you on your laptop, PDA, or your hard drive at home. If you must maintain sensitive information on your laptop, PDA, cell phone, or home computers, at least keep it in an encrypted file.

15. **No one is immune to identity theft.**
   True—Anyone who has a Social Security number or biometric information that is stored in a government or commercial database is a potential target. American babies receive an Social Security number almost immediately after birth. (We've heard from many parents who learned that their child's identity was stolen at an early age.) When people die, their Social Security

number may be used by a con artist to impersonate that person for financial gain or to avoid prosecution. Even persons with a bad credit rating may find themselves victims of criminal identity theft.

Now that you've had a chance to check your answers, you're ready to examine how your everyday information-handling habits either protect you or expose you as a target for identity thieves. If you are concerned, rest assured that you'll have greater peace of mind when you finish reading *Safeguard Your Identity*.

Yes, It *Can* Happen to You!

"When evil minded people plot,
good minded people must prepare."

— Martin Luther King, Jr.

Imagine this: The phone rings, and a collection agency demands that you pay past-due accounts for merchandise you never ordered. The supermarket starts refusing your checks, claiming you have a history of bouncing them. How can this be happening? You have a perfect credit record and you always pay bills on time. Then comes the final blow; you apply for a new job and the company denies you the position saying they can't hire someone with a criminal record—yet you've never even been arrested! What has happened? Unfortunately, someone has stolen your identity.

The crime of identity theft has become a plague in our society. A recent survey by the Federal Trade Commission (FTC) found that more than 9.9 million people became victims of identity theft in one year! According to the FTC, consumer victims (in 2003) lost over $5 billion, and spent over 300 million hours to regain their identity. Businesses lost $48 billion.

Using a variety of methods, criminals steal credit card numbers, driver's license numbers, Social Security numbers, ATM cards, healthcare cards, telephone calling cards, and other key pieces of personal identification. They use this information to impersonate their victims, spending as much money as they can in as short a time as possible before moving on to someone else's name and profile or account information. But they can do more than just spend money. Anything you can do with your identity, your evil impostor can do: They can become legal citizens; use your professional license; work under your name and Social Security number to avoid paying taxes; receive healthcare; commit various crimes that leave you with a criminal record; and more. Fraudsters can even commit terrorist acts while using your identity. Over one-half of the 9/11 terrorists committed identity theft to get credit cards, rent apartments, lease cars, receive pilot lessons, and avoid suspicion.

As far as financial identity fraud is concerned, however, there is some good news. Thanks to federal law, victims of credit and banking fraud are generally liable for no more than the first $50 of the loss. In fact, in most cases victims are not required to pay any part of credit card theft. This isn't always the case with check and debit card fraud, but there are federal laws that provide some protection from loss.

Even though victims rarely get saddled with paying their imposters' bills, they are often left with a poor credit profile and must spend months, sometimes years, regaining their financial health. In the meantime, they have difficulty writing checks, obtaining loans, renting apartments, buying houses and even getting hired. Plus, identity theft victims receive little help from the authorities and agencies as they attempt to untangle the web of deception that has allowed another person to impersonate them.

The tips provided in this book will help you reduce your chances of becoming a victim of identity theft. You can use the information to perform your own personal privacy audit to help you protect yourself from the epidemic of identity theft. The information-handling practices we advocate for both households and businesses will make it more difficult for imposters to obtain the information required to commit this crime. And if you should become a victim of identity theft, something I sincerely hope will never happen, this book provides you with the roadmap to find your way back to financial health.

As you read through the book, you may notice that I occasionally repeat certain warnings and recommendations—that's because I feel some ideas are worth repeating.

Please know that adopting the information management strategy in this book will put you less at risk for becoming a victim of identity theft. What about total prevention? Until systemic changes occur in the credit industry, and in laws that govern financial institutions, and in the ways both government agencies and businesses assign and use Social Security numbers, biometric information (i.e., fingerprints), and other identifiers, completely eradicating this insidious crime will be difficult. You'll see why it's important to become an advocate for corrective laws, proper information-handling approaches, and improved industry privacy practices. In this age of instantaneous information transfer, your privacy (defined as the ability to control how your personal information is used, bought, sold, and shared) is diminishing at light speed. By the time you finish reading this book, you'll be empowered to become an agent for positive changes to protect your identity, your security, and your privacy. Use the tips in this guide to help you develop your own privacy protection plan, and stick to it. This will require you, your family, your friends, and colleagues to change old habits and adopt new ones. Use the recommendations in this book as Your Personal Privacy Audit so you can Safeguard Your Identity.

We value your ideas and suggestions, so please visit the Identity Theft Prevention and Survival website at **www.identitytheft.org**, and e-mail us your comments. Thank you for choosing this book, I hope it provides you with an easy way to take positive steps to protect your most valuable asset, your identity!

Chapter One

The Red Convertible I Never Owned

"Nothing in life is to be feared. It is only to be understood."

—Marie Curie

What Is Identity Theft And How Does It Happen?

When a woman I never knew took my identity in 1996, I was terrified. My evil-twin stole over $50,000 in my name, used my good reputation and credit to buy a red convertible; totaled a rental car for which I was sued; and worse yet, assumed my profession as an attorney, distributing business cards with my name on them. At that time, there were no laws making identity theft a crime against the victim; the law considered the creditor the real victim. I had to forge my way through the identity theft jungle to understand what was happening. Only then could I rectify the nightmare, and protect myself from the same thing occurring again. Although you may have seen horror stories about this crime on television, and you may be fearful of it happening to you—since no one is immune—once you understand what it is, and learn corrective measures to deal with it, you will rest easier. My goal in this book is to help you understand your vulnerability, and give you tools to minimize your risk.

Before you can protect yourself from the crime of identity theft, you've got to learn just exactly what it is and how it can happen. Simply put, you become a victim of identity theft when someone uses your personal identifiers, like your name, Social Security number, and other personal information, even a fingerprint, without your permission so they can impersonate you to commit fraud.

Imposters will steal your identity for four main reasons—financial gain; to avoid arrest or prosecution for crimes they commit; for revenge or retaliation; and for acts of terrorism. Following are examples of each type of identity theft, but remember, there is no limit to the creativity of these impostors. Whatever you can do or obtain with your identity, your impersonator can also do as your "clone."

Financial Gain

John and Sue Smith were in the process of buying their first house, when John's credit reports showed him as being delinquent on payments for credit accounts that were not his. Their credit report showed outstanding bills of $35,000 for accounts from Citibank Credit Card Company, Bank One, and Capital One. Upset and frustrated, they feared this damage to their credit cost them their dream of owning a house. Worse, their apartment lease ended and the landlord rented their unit to other renters. John and Sue began to worry that they would have no place to live. This young couple had fallen victim to identity theft for financial gain, and their lives had been thrown into crisis.

In our easy-credit society, where billions of pre-approved credit offers arrive in American mailboxes every day, where companies pass out credit cards like candy on Halloween, using your good name and credit is an easy way for criminally-minded persons to steal from innocent, good people like you. With this "faceless crime," a perpetrator doesn't have to use a gun or ever meet the victim; all he or she needs is a bit of information. Right now the key to the kingdom of identity theft is the Social Security number. But in the near future it could even be a fingerprint, an iris scan, or another unique "piece of your body" called biometric information that is transferred electronically via the Internet. The game is the same—to use your good reputation to commit fraud.

Greed leads fraudsters to adopt very creative ways of using your identity. Not only can the thieves obtain credit cards using your information, but they can siphon money from your bank accounts, investment accounts, trust funds, college accounts, retirement plans, get life insurance in your name (and make themselves the beneficiary), secure medical services, have babies using your health insurance, steal your disability payments or Social Security checks, receive unemployment compensation, get your tax refund, or even file bankruptcy using your identity. The creative charlatan can do anything as your evil-twin. Here is another example of a couple that I spoke with many times as they lived through identity theft hell.

George and Ida Jones, a retired military couple living in Virginia, experienced what they call a living nightmare. For more than two years, an identity thief had used their names and Social Security numbers to open up 30 credit accounts, making purchases totaling more than $100,000. The imposter had also purchased a Jeep Cherokee. The Jones family had been hounded almost daily by collection agencies. They even had a civil suit filed against them *for nonpayment of a furniture bill. They think the imposter was able to obtain their Social Security numbers from their military ID cards, which display the number.*

The Jones and Smith families (names are changed to protect their privacy) are victims of one of the fastest-growing crimes of our time. The Federal Bureau of Investigation (FBI) reports that one in five adults has been victimized by some form of identity theft. Indeed, identity theft is increasing at epidemic proportions and financial reward is the leading reason for this crime. Below are examples of the top five types of financial hoaxes that fraudsters can commit using your identity:

1. **Credit card fraud**

   Mary opened her credit card billing statement and saw $2,000 worth of charges she didn't recognize—all orders for merchandise and gasoline in another state. Yet her credit card was still in her wallet. She discovered she'd been skimmed. It may have happened at a restaurant when the fraudster-waiter smiled at her, took her credit card, then ran it through a skimmer, which copied the information imbedded in the magnetic strip on the back of the card. After capturing the information into the skimmer device, he probably downloaded the information onto his computer and sent the information to friends who created fraudulent credit cards duplicating Mary's card.

   Steve discovered someone had opened seven new credit card accounts in his name in a city three hours from his home. He believes that when he refinanced his home, a "dirty employee" at the lender or the escrow office took his financial information to commit the fraud.

2. **Utility theft**

   Laura, in Utah, began to receive collection calls regarding delinquent phone accounts in California. She learned that several men in a penal institution in California had used her Social Security number, but not her name, to open up phone accounts. Her Social Security number is now associated with several men's names and many different telephone numbers.

3. **Bank swindles**

   Stacy, a college student, learned that her impostor deposited $8,000 worth of phony checks into her checking account, and then proceeded to use the checking account to buy goods and services. All of Stacy's own checks bounced, and her bank refused to help her, accusing her of conspiracy.

4. **Employment deception**

   José, a legal citizen was injured on the job. When he applied for worker's compensation payments, he was told that he was not eligible since he was already receiving payments in another county in his state.

   Barbara's impostor, her cousin (who had a felony conviction), decided to use Barbara's résumé and identification to work as a teacher in another state.

5. **Counterfeit loans**

   Jack and Jane paid off and closed an equity line of credit on their home only to find that impostors had re-opened the account and written checks for $100,000 over the limit of the credit line.

   Monetary profit was the key motivator for the impersonators

listed above, but there are other reasons why someone may impersonate you. Read on.

Criminal Identity Theft; Avoiding Arrest or Prosecution

Brian, a financial analyst, learned that his friend's brother, Robert, who has similar physical features, had used Brian's name when he was arrested for various criminal offenses. Brian recently called us in a panic when he learned that Robert was also a sex offender.

Imagine this: You're sitting at your desk at work and two law enforcement officers approach you to ask for your identification. They begin to interrogate you, and then, in front of your colleagues, tell you that they have a warrant for your arrest; they handcuff you and take you to the police station. Once there, you learn someone has used your identity to commit a crime that you know nothing about. Although cleaning up your financial profile after identity theft is time-consuming and frustrating, it's far more frightening, and challenging, to clear a criminal record!

Revenge: Retaliation

Georgia rebuffed the advances of a security guard who worked at her building. To retaliate, the guard entered cyberspace and pretended to be Georgia, describing in detail in various chat rooms Georgia's alleged fantasies of being raped. Georgia, who didn't own a computer, had no idea what this man had done until to her horror, various "suitors" arrived at her door. The case was later prosecuted as a cyber crime.

Terrorism

Over half of the terrorists who committed the atrocious acts of 9/11 committed identity theft. In fact, they committed all three previous types of theft.

- They wanted financial gain; so they used fraudulent identities to obtain credit cards, cell phones, hotel rooms, and even flying lessons.
- Several of the terrorists were known to authorities, so they avoided apprehension by assuming someone else's identity.
- Lastly, and more disturbing, they committed identity theft to get revenge against our country.

So, identity theft is not just about you and me spending hundreds of hours to regain our lives; it is also about recognizing that identity theft may allow evil-minded persons to murder our citizens, commit terrorist acts, and jeopardize our country's safety and freedom.

How Do Thieves Steal Your Identity?

In this age of instant credit and pre-approved credit offers, identity thieves require little more than your name and Social Security number, plus your date of birth if they get lucky, to assume your identity. These fraudsters are skillful at using a variety of low-tech and high-tech methods to obtain your personal information.

Stealing wallets and purses is the old-fashioned way for thieves to take on your identity. While that still happens, imposters employ many other methods to obtain the bits and pieces of information that identify you. We still find that most information is stolen in the real world, but it's used extensively in the virtual world of the Internet.

Thieves steal mail from mailboxes to obtain bank and credit card statements, pre-approved credit offers, utility statements, driver's license numbers, Social Security numbers, and tax information. They may pose as you and report an address change in order to divert your mail, including those ubiquitous pre-approved offers of credit, to their own address—or more likely, to a drop box. At the same time, they report a lost credit card and order a new one. Federal law requires credit card companies to verify any address change, but often it just doesn't happen.

Mary didn't know anything was amiss until she realized she wasn't receiving her favorite magazine. Her mail had been diverted from her California home to a New York address. The identity thieves, members of a crime ring, forged her name on pre-approved credit application forms, raided her bank accounts, and destroyed her credit rating.

Identity thieves dumpster dive to fish un-shredded loan and credit card applications from the trash of households and businesses.

A large insurance company moved its headquarters and discarded hundreds of boxes of their customers' sensitive information without bothering to shred or burn the information. Hundreds of customers became victims of fraud.

They might access your credit report fraudulently by posing as an employer, loan officer, or landlord. Or they might illicitly obtain Social Security numbers and credit information while actually employed by a company with access to a credit bureau database.

Several employees at an automobile dealership ordered the credit reports of potential car buyers, and sold the printed financial profiles to gangs who stole the unsuspecting customers' identities.

They scam you through e-mail or regular mail or by phone, pretending to be a legitimate agency or company asking for your personal data.

Fraudsters sent e-mails to AOL customers stating that their account information had to be updated – believing the e-mails to be authentic, many individuals gave their credit card numbers and personal information, and suffered the loss of their identity.

A very common method is to gain insider access to an agency or company's personnel files, critical databases maintained by the company, which contain Social Security numbers, dates of birth, biometric information, and other sensitive information.

In June 2004 a computer was stolen containing 145,000 UCLA blood donors' social security numbers, birthdates and other personal information.

Business record theft is a growing threat. It can be as simple as stealing files or a computer, or it can be sophisticated electronic hacking by fraudsters living in a foreign country, thousands of miles away.

A hacker stole 300,000 credit card numbers from the Internet Retailer CD Universe and then posted 25,000 of them on a website when a $100,000 ransom was not paid.

They use personal information they find about you in chat rooms, e-mails, and from information brokers on the Internet.

In May of 2004 a man was convicted of sending 850 million junk e-mails through accounts he opened with stolen identities after the Internet service provider Earthlink, Inc won a $16.4 million judgment in court against him—so this was retaliation.

❖

A member of a notorious crime ring was employed temporarily at a large corporation. He downloaded the employee list containing Social Security numbers and dates of birth, then provided this information to members of the ring. One by one, the employees' identities were used to fraudulently obtain credit. The employees didn't know about it until they started sharing stories about being hounded by creditors and collection agencies for purchases they did not make. It wasn't until much later that the human resources department confessed to having known about the theft. Company officials didn't want to tell the employees and cause them to panic.

(Some states, like California, require that companies that experience a security breach of unencrypted files of sensitive information notify all potential victims of the breach, so that they may protect themselves with a fraud alert. Federal guidelines for financial institutions encourage notification as well.)

Sadly, some identity thieves obtain in-home access to personal documents. They might be relatives or friends, roommates, household workers, home-healthcare providers, or spouses going through a divorce who hold a grudge. Worse yet, sons and daughters do this to elderly parents, and some parents steal the identities of their children. While we hate to think of those closest to us committing identity theft, it is more common than you might think.

These days, we are also seeing more high-tech identity theft via the Internet. Fee-based computer services sell Social Security numbers and other identifying information for as little as $25. Although reputable information vendors are limiting access to Social Security numbers, the Net is the Wild West of the information age, and is virtually impossible to regulate.

Another form of high-tech thievery is hacking into the records of Web-based businesses or governmental entities that don't encrypt their files.

Most victims of identity theft have no clue how the imposter obtained their identifying information. The victim rarely meets his impersonator, and in most cases, because law enforcement hasn't the resources to investigate, the crime goes unsolved. The fraudster is free to find new targets.

Watch out for faulty information-handling practices

As if protecting your identity from theft wasn't already a challenge, it seems that some merchants, agencies, and banks seem to almost open the door for identity thieves to commit fraud. When was the last time a merchant closely examined the signature on your credit card? How many businesses fail to properly dispose of documents by shredding? How many businesses don't bother to lock up filing cabinets containing your personal data? What steps do companies take to authenticate their customers? The financial industry is in the best position to prevent the crime, but often, because untrained employees are eager to issue new credit cards and loans, the proper verification doesn't take place.

Many banks still require the last four digits of the Social Security number as the default PIN for ATM cards and telephone banking access. Many health and life insurance companies use the Social Security number as the insurance account number and emblazon it on each policyholder's card, which must then be carried in the wallet. Medicare cards display the Social Security number. Many colleges and universities still use the Social Security number as the student ID, even posting grades by this number. In a few states, the Social Security number is still the driver's license number. All these uses of our allegedly unique identifier put you and me at risk. The trend toward authentication and verification using biometric information, such as your fingerprint or iris scan, is lauded as a panacea; however, accuracy for that data is not wholly reliable and if the minimum level of protection for that sensitive data is comparable to the protections now used for the Social Security number, victims will have far more problems proving who they are if defrauded using a unique body identifier.

No respect ... and no help: What happens to victims of identity theft?

Even though each identity fraud case is different, the experiences of all victims are all too similar.

Victims get little or no help from the agencies and companies who allowed the personal identifying information to be used fraudulently in the first place.

Law enforcement rarely gets involved. Identity theft occurs far too often for them to handle it all, although many police departments are expanding their financial fraud departments. Some police departments still will not issue a police report to victims, declaring the bank the true victim due to its, not the victim's, monetary loss. But federal laws and most state laws (see Laws at the end of this book) make identity theft a crime, which encourages law enforcement to make a police report. Plus, federal law (The Fair Credit Report Act) requires a police report or an "identity theft report" for the victim to clear his name with the credit reporting agencies and the credit grantors.

Many victims report difficulty reaching the credit bureaus or getting responses in writing. They also describe abusive and rude treatment by some creditors and debt collectors and government agencies.

Victims must spend a great deal of time regaining their financial health. They typically must take days off work to make the necessary phone calls, write letters, and get affidavits notarized. Victims can be saddled with this situation for months, even years. The Identity Theft Resource Center surveyed victims and found that they average 600 hours each in time spent to clear their names. (**www.idtheftcenter.org**) (See the 2003 report.) Plus, this all costs money as well.

A most disastrous scenario occurs when the thief commits crimes in the victim's name and the victim is arrested and/or required to stand trial for a crime he or she did not commit.

Another horrific situation arises when the imposter works under the victim's name and Social Security number. The earnings show on the victim's Social Security Administration account. Eventually, the Internal Revenue Service investigates the victim for under-reporting income.

Essentially, the entire burden of this crime is placed on the shoulders of the victims, often leaving them emotionally scarred. They feel violated and helpless—and very angry. After all, they may be unable to obtain credit, get a mortgage, rent an apartment, or acquire a job—all because an imposter's bad credit history or worse yet, a false criminal background is recorded in myriad databases, ruining their good name. When the identity theft includes criminal charges or revenge, the restoration of the victim's normal life can take a lifetime.

How can you protect yourself from falling victim to this devious crime? How can the business or organization you work for or deal with establish high quality information-handling practices to prevent identity theft from happening to its clients, customers, and employees? We'll cover all these important topics in Chapters Two, Three, and Four—the heart of this book.

To make this guide user-friendly, we've used the list approach. Consider these bullets and points as action items, and use them as your personal privacy audit to assess your present vulnerability. We suggest committing to implementing only one or two pages at a time, and then incorporating the suggestions into your everyday life to Safeguard Your Identity.

Chapter Two

It Takes More Than a Four-Leaf Clover: How to Protect Your Personal Identity

"The fantastic advances in the field of communication constitute a grave danger to the privacy of the individual."

—Earl Warren (1871-1974), American jurist, chief justice of U. S. Supreme Court

Susan, a single businesswoman travels a great deal for business. For a couple of years her next-door neighbor, Don, would pet sit her dog. Using a key to Susan's townhome, he would let himself in to feed and walk Sparky, and take in the mail while Susan was out of town. One evening Susan returned early to find Don at work on her computer; at the time she wasn't concerned. Then she began to notice that, although he had recently been laid off from his job, he was buying new "toys"—a motorcycle and electronic equipment. In fact, Don soon moved out of state. Collection agencies began to call Susan, and money disappeared from her checking account. What had happened? Susan's unlocked desk had a notebook with all of her on-line banking passwords and personal information, including her Social Security number. Her trust in people was shattered, and she is now living in identity theft hell.

If Susan had known to take action in the following 12 areas, she might have reduced her chances of becoming a victim of identity theft. Use the following information as a checklist to help you assess your own vulnerability, and as a guide to help you develop your own privacy protection strategy. This chapter, and those that follow, will help you gauge your safety on two levels—your personal life and your life interacting in the outside world. Chapter Two and Three deal with personal protection, and Chapter Four discusses your experiences with businesses, government agencies, and in the workplace; basically, you can evaluate how well you are shielded when interacting in your daily activities inside / outside your home.

Some of the steps in this chapter may seem challenging, or burdensome, but as you know by now, the risks are high and a minor inconvenience may be a small price to pay to guard your identity. Take one tip at a time to implement your own strategy to Safeguard Your Identity.

Bear in mind that no matter how many times you opt-out, no matter how many letters you send, no matter how careful you are with your Social Security and credit card numbers, no matter how many documents you shred or passwords you memorize, nothing will guarantee that a criminal won't get access to your information in our increasingly data-saturated society. We live in an age where information can be retrieved easily in the real world or the virtual world, and then can be shipped anywhere on earth by computer in a nanosecond. So, criminals do have an advantage, but we can empower ourselves to level the playing field.

If you take actions now to defend yourself, you'll become less of an easy target.

Personal Identity Theft Safety Measures

1. Safely store and discard personal information.

Contrary to popular belief, most identity thieves steal information about you the old-fashioned way . . . "off-line," not from your computer. But the reason we have such an epidemic of this crime is because thieves can use the information so easily and quickly on the Internet, where vendors have no face-to-face interaction with buyers. Your evil-twin can make purchases with your credit card from the seclusion of his bedroom in another state or a far off country. To protect yourself from this:

- **Keep your financial records under lock and key, at home and while traveling.**
  Burglars may be more interested in your bank and credit card information than in your VCR. Furthermore, you'd be surprised at how many cases of identity theft involve a perpetrator known to the victim: a relative, client, roommate, cleaning service, tenant or someone else who has easy access to the victim's house and to his or her account numbers, Social Security number, and driver's license number. Don't leave such information in plain view in your home, car, or on your computer.

  Invest in some locking file cabinets for your confidential documents. Put padlocks on the doors of any closets that contain boxes of old tax returns and financial statements. Secure briefcases containing private documents (with a locking device and alarm) in your locked trunk. When using a valet, provide a key that doesn't open the trunk. Consider a burglar alarm for your home and automobile (make sure you place a sticker on your window to warn potential thieves of the alarm—it may just frighten them away). And think about getting a dog with a loud bark to ward off unwanted visitors!

- **Buy and use a shredder.**
  Any papers you don't need to keep that contain private information should be destroyed. For a small investment, you can purchase a shredder to destroy those old records, and all pre-approved credit applications and convenience checks. (The checks that your credit card company sends you that only require a signature). In fact, write to your credit card companies and ask them not to send you those checks, which often arrive attached to your billing statement. Fraudsters can use those "hot checks" very easily. The Postal Inspector's office told us that 35 percent of those convenience checks are used fraudulently. So stop them from coming in your mail. For security reasons, make sure you use a crosscut shredder that cuts paper into small dots, virtually impossible to reconstruct.

- **Be careful of "dumpster divers."**
  Your trash can tell a lot about you—sometimes too much. Make sure that you don't throw away anything that someone could use to assume your identity: credit card , checking account, or investment account statements, insurance policies, credit-card receipts, old tax returns, escrow documents, or brokerage statements. Even utility statements provide enough information to enable a hoaxer to open utility accounts in another location. Anything that contains your financial or confidential information must be completely destroyed or it could destroy your finances.

- **Take extra precautions when you move or do spring cleaning**
  When moving, take your old files of tax returns, loan applications, escrow documents and all other old confidential files and burn or shred them. To make it easier, call a bonded shredding service to take your boxes full of sensitive documents and

pulverize them. Better yet, some services will bring a shredding truck to disintegrate your boxes of data right in your driveway, and then you can rest assured that your sensitive data has truly been destroyed.

- **Tell others who fax to your home not to send confidential information in a fax to you unless they call first to confirm that you are there to receive it.**
  If guests or babysitters are in your home when faxes arrive, they may retrieve this information without your knowledge, to your detriment.

- **Quiz every firm or organization—banks, brokerages, doctors' offices, accountants, lawyers and even your own employer—about what they do with your private information.**
  Many companies you deal with still are not conscious of the risks of identity theft and fail to recognize the privacy issues. Unfortunately, identity theft is often caused by shoddy information handling practices. When dealing with merchants, vendors and professionals, insist that they guard your personal information, secure data in locked files, and shred before putting your documents in the trash. Several states require companies to completely destroy sensitive documents before discarding. California, Wisconsin, and Georgia were the first to pass document destruction laws. Find out what security procedures the offices you deal with have in place to protect your files both online and off-line. We'll discuss this more in Chapter Three.

- **Don't co-sign for car loans, credit cards, and other credit with a friend or adult child.**
  Once you do this, they may use your information to apply for new accounts using your name. Or, they may use the former co-signed agreement to obtain new accounts, loans etc. We've

helped many individuals who were victimized by their own children in this way. Sad, but it happens.

2. Managing your credit cards.

- **Get credit cards with your picture on them.**
  Not all credit card issuers will do this, but some will. Shop around.

- **When you order new credit cards or your current ones are expiring, keep an eye on the calendar.**
  Be alert when a new card ought to be arriving. If it doesn't arrive when you expect it, call the credit card issuer immediately and find out if the card was sent. If it was sent more than 10 days before your call, but you still haven't received it, cancel it at once.

- **Mark your calendar for credit card bills.**
  If you haven't received your billing statement, you may find out that it was sent to an imposter.

- **Put new passwords on all your financial accounts.**
  This may be bothersome and may not win you friends with the bank or your creditors, but it's important. Make it something other than your mother's maiden name, a pet's name, or the name of someone in your family. If you think you might forget the password, ask if the bank or creditor will record a question it can ask to help you remember. Consider using at least eight letters.

- **Cancel all credit cards that you haven't used in six months.**
  If you don't pare down your unused cards, you might as well be carrying around dynamite while waiting for a match. If you carry a little-used card, you are not likely to quickly notice if

it's lost or stolen. Also, if the thief has your credit report, he or she has notice of an account that is ripe for extensive use. Thus, you're giving a thief a big head start. Before discarding any cards, call to cancel and then cut the canceled cards into small pieces and render the numbers unreadable.

- **Monitor all statements from every credit card and bank.** If there's anything on the statement you don't recall buying, call the credit grantor to verify that the debt is truly yours. If it's not yours, cancel the card and get a new account number using a unique password.
- **Carefully review all bank statements and financial statements.**
  Many victims learn too late that money was stolen by fraudsters, using their checks or debit cards.
- **Don't put your address, telephone number, or driver's license number on the credit card slip from restaurants or stores.**
  In fact, this practice is a violation of law in many states. It is also contrary to most credit card companies' policies. Of course, for ordering by mail you will need to provide complete address information on the order form. But you don't need to write your driver's license or Social Security number on the order form.
- **Don't put your credit card account numbers on the Internet (except on a secure site). In general, be careful who you give those numbers to.**
  Guard those numbers zealously. Never give out a credit card number unless you have a trusted business relationship with the company, and you call them, not vice versa. If you shop on the Internet, use a secure browser that encrypts or scrambles account information, or place your order by telephone, fax,

or mail. Make sure the Internet merchant stores credit account data in encrypted form. Only use a secure browser. Look for the lock at the bottom of your computer screen.

- **Don't allow a merchant to print your credit card number on checks.**
  It's against the law in many states. With your credit card number and bank account number all in one place, an identity thief can do a lot of damage.

- **If you think you've misplaced or lost a credit card, assume the worst.**
  Call the issuing bank immediately. As Allan Trosclair, a former FBI agent and former vice president of fraud control at Visa USA, puts it: "If you think you lost it [your credit card] around the house, don't spend three or four days looking for it. The bad guys use it up in two days. So call immediately, don't take the chance." It costs the banks about $125 to issue a new card, he said, "But they'd rather do that than have a couple hundred thousand dollars of fraud on your account."

- **Keep a list of all your credit cards and bank accounts.**
  Include the account numbers, expiration dates, and phone numbers of the issuers' customer service departments. Update the list as needed and keep it in a secure place so you can quickly contact your creditors if your cards are lost or stolen. Don't keep this information on your computer or PDA. Keep it on a CD and hard copy. Then lock it in a secure filing cabinet. Make Xerox copies of each card and store these in a locked file.

  Jeff Levy, computer expert and host of a syndicated computer talk radio show tells us, "Avoid storing your personal information on your computer. Things that require your name and your Social Security information should never be kept on your hard drive." Quicken, Microsoft Money, and other programs that track our financial information all allow us to store data on CDs, not on the hard drive.

For Internet users who travel extensively, "Create a list of all your credit card companies (don't list the account numbers) with the toll-free numbers. Save it in a file folder with a Web-based e-mail account like Yahoo. This will provide you instant access to your credit card companies to cancel your accounts in the event of loss or theft of your wallet, even when you are away from home. As an alternative, sign up for a service (with your credit card company) that will cancel all your cards with one call.

3. Protecting your financial transactions.

- **Use checks only when necessary.**
  You are safer using a credit card to buy groceries, gas, products and services than you are using a check.

- **Don't print your Social Security number on your checks.**
  Don't allow merchants to write it on checks, either. Retailers don't need it—thieves do. Also, don't print your Social Security number on your business cards, address labels, invoices, or other identifying information. Try to convince your employer to follow the same precautions.

- **Don't print your telephone number or full name on your checks.**
  Put your initials and last name on your checks. If a merchant asks you for your phone number, you can decide to add it at that time.

- **When you order new checks, have them delivered to your local bank branch, not to your home.**

Boxes of blank checks are readily recognizable and an easy target for mail thieves.

- **Don't give your checking account number to people you don't know.**
  Be equally suspicious if they claim they're from the bank.

- **Take precautions against illegitimate access to your accounts.**
  Write to your bank and ask them to notify you in writing if someone requests your records.

- **Store cancelled checks in a locked file.**
  When you discard them, shred or burn them. Your checking account numbers can be used to impersonate you.

- **Consider canceling your ATM debit card with the Visa / MasterCard logo. Use a regular ATM card instead.**
  It's safer to use a credit card than an ATM debit with a Visa / MasterCard logo. If your debit card is used without your authorization, the money is directly withdrawn from your bank account. If someone uses your credit card, you have the opportunity to dispute the charges before you pay the bill. All you need is a regular ATM card to get cash or make deposits anywhere in the world. For purchases use a normal credit card.

4. Protect information by phone.

- **Establish an unpublished phone number so that your name and home address won't be in the phone book and so you'll be removed from reverse directories.**
  Make sure you also opt-out of having your cell phone listed in a 411 directory.

- **Block your phone number from showing up on Caller ID (Order this option with your telephone provider.)**
  Your number will not show on Caller ID if you have indicated this option with your local phone carrier. You'll need to input *82 to unblock your number to place a call to numbers that do not accept blocked calls. Be aware this will disclose your phone number when necessary.

- **Never give out any personal information over the phone to someone you don't know.**
  If someone tells you he or she represents a credit grantor of yours, or a government agency, call the person at a telephone number that you know is the true number and ask for that person. Even then, provide only information that you believe is absolutely necessary. Only give your credit card on the phone when you make the call to a trusted number.

- **Tell your children not to give out information to anyone on the phone, at the door, or on the Internet.**
  Children are very trusting and inexperienced; they need your guidance to protect simple personal information.

- **Check to see who is listening when sharing confidential information on a speakerphone.**
  Persons who could use the information to commit fraud may overhear you.

5. Defend yourself against identity theft when using cell phone.

- **If your wireless phone is lost or stolen, immediately de-activate it.**
  If you find it within a few days, it can be re-activated.

- **To be safe, don't give out personal, financial, or confiden-**

tial data while on your wireless phone.
Current cellular phones are much more secure than the old-style analog phones. However, our cell phone communications can be unscrambled by law enforcement and techies. Also, some cell phones can be used as microphones and used to eavesdrop on conversations. Check your credit reports for cellular service inquiries.

Cell phone fraud has become epidemic. A fraudster will open an account in your name with your Social Security number, and the bills will be sent to the impostor's address. When no bills are paid, the victim learns of this account from collection companies demanding payment. Here are some things you can do to minimize your risk:

- **Carefully monitor your cell phone bills thoroughly each month: Look for phone calls you did not make and report them immediately to the phone carrier.**
- **Check your credit reports to see if any inquiries were made by cell phone companies (this would alert you that someone has applied for a cell phone in your name).**
- **Unless you are traveling overseas, contact your cell phone carrier and ask that the phone be limited to calls within the United States.**
- **When you aren't using your phone, use the phone's locking feature: Don't let others borrow your phone, and keep it in your possession at all times when you are away from home. If you are on vacation, lock your cell phone in the hotel safe. When you're at home, and not using the phone, secure it in a locked drawer.**
- **Never give out confidential or financial information**

over a wireless or cordless phone: Persons with scanners may be able to listen in on your conversations when you least expect it. Your wireless transmissions are not secure. It is best to use a "landline" for confidential communications.

- **When using a wireless phone in a public place, be careful to speak quietly, and move to a secluded area when speaking about your sensitive information: Many people speak louder than normal when using a wireless phone. It's easy to eavesdrop on cell phone users' calls at a restaurant or standing in line for a theatre.**

6. Guard your identity when using other wireless devices.

In this age of high-tech gadgets, we find many wireless devices make our lives easier and more enjoyable, but we tend to be oblivious to their dangers and don't know how to protect ourselves. The following devices operate on radio frequencies that can be picked up by radio scanners, cordless phones, and other monitors; be aware when using these devices:

Walkie-Talkies: Families use these to communicate all the time on vacation, at festivals and any place where it's easy to lose each other. But if you aren't careful, you may lose your identity.

Home intercom systems: Make sure the intercom is off when sharing confidential information.

Baby monitors: Consider using the wired version to be more secure. Neighbors can pick up conversations on baby monitors.

Wireless microphones: Professional speakers, entertainers, and others use these. The information shared can be transmitted, so be mindful of the sensitive information shared at gatherings.

Wireless video cameras: Many security-minded people have installed these devices to provide security. The camera sends the images to be viewed on a computer or TV, but these devices are easy to monitor by criminals who may be viewing the images as well. Consider using wired cameras and tapes for safety.

Airplane wireless phones: These are vulnerable to radio scanners. When using airplane phones, others around you can also hear your conversations. Wait to use a landline to have confidential conversations.

7. Secure your Personal Data Assistant (PDA).

People use these devices to check e-mail, surf the web, maintain calendar and contact files, and some people use them to store their credit card numbers and other sensitive information. The biggest threats to those of us concerned with identity theft are the following:

- Theft of the PDA itself (especially if it contains sensitive data)
- Password Theft
- Viruses and data corruption
- Wireless vulnerabilities.

As we suggest for wireless connection to the Internet, don't keep sensitive information on the PDA. If you choose to keep private information on your PDA, there are encryption solutions. Many people don't like to use these because they slow down the use of the device.

- **Encrypt data**
  If you have sensitive information stored on any wireless device, you should encrypt the data and access should be password protected.

- **If you are transmitting wirelessly, then ensure proper user / device authentication before transmission.**
  Encrypt data during the transmission and maintain an audit trail.

- **To protect data if the PDA is lost or stolen, utilize user ID and Password level security.**
  To find out more on how to protect yourself with wireless devices, and access reviews of Internet security products, including wireless computer networks and PDAs, visit the Web at **www.firewallguide.com / index.htm**. Protect your mail and mailbox.

8. Protect your mail.

- **Don't mail checks from your home mailbox.**
  When you pay your bills, make the effort to drop them off at the post office. If you leave them as outgoing mail for the letter carrier, you create an easy target for a thief who can learn a great deal about you from that handful of envelopes. Also, it's not hard for a crook to steal a check, acid wash the name of the recipient, and make himself or herself the payee.

  Consider using an alternate means of paying bills. Pay-by-phone, initiated from your own bank, is a secure transaction. The bank sends the payment electronically or by draft to the payee. You won't have to use your checks!

- **Get a post office box or a locked residential mailbox.**
  Theft of mail is so easy—and so potentially ruinous to your identity. This is a simple precaution that pays big dividends in peace of mind.

- **Don't throw away pre-approved offers that you receive in the mail.**

Some privacy advocates suggest marking the mail "refused, return to sender." We suggest shredding and opting out instead.

9. Review, access, and correct your credit reports.

- **Order your credit report from all three major credit-reporting agencies (CRAs) at least two times a year.**
  You are entitled to one free credit report from each of the three major credit-reporting agencies per year (1-877-322-8228). We suggest you get them twice a year, or sign up for a credit monitoring service that accesses all three companies.

  Look for any debts you don't recognize and any credit inquiries that don't look familiar. For example, look closely for possible inquiries by a tenant screening company, or by a company that you don't recognize. Unfamiliar inquiries might mean someone has used your name to rent property—which could eventually lead to an eviction or other negative information being added to your report. If there are errors, make sure you immediately write to the CRA to have the items corrected or removed. Now you can even write to the companies via e-mail.

  To order your credit report, contact the following agencies:

  Equifax: **www.equifax.com** or phone 800-685-1111
  Experian: **www.experian.com** or phone 888-397-3742
  TransUnion: **www.transunion.com** or phone 800-888-4213

- **Immediately correct all mistakes on your credit reports in writing.**
  Send a letter to the credit-reporting agencies by certified mail, return receipt requested, identifying the mistakes item by item on a copy of the credit report. You should hear from each agency within 30 days (mark you calendar). A study performed in June, 2004, by the U.S. Public Interest Research Group (USPIRG),

found that 79 percent of the credit reports analyzed had errors; one in four (25%) were severe enough for consumers to be denied credit, a loan, an apartment, or a job.

Think of your credit report as a snapshot. By the time you request and receive it, it has probably changed, because new information is being added all the time. The fact that it's good today doesn't mean it's going to be good tomorrow or the next day. So, check it often, at least two times a year. It should be sent to you at no cost if you have been denied credit, are indigent, or if you are a victim of identity theft. It's best to check all three companies since they don't all have the same data. Before you apply for a job or credit, make sure you check your profile for errors and to raise your score.

10. Block your name from marketing lists.

- **Protect your financial privacy**
  Financial companies are required by law to mail a privacy notice to you once a year under the Federal Financial Modernization Act. Don' t throw out those privacy brochures or letters, write or call the number provided in the notices and stop your financial institutions from selling your personal information or sharing it with third parties. Some companies will also allow you to opt out of sharing information with affiliates. California and North Dakota have passed more stringent privacy laws, which require financial institutions to get prior permission before selling / sharing your information with third parties (called opt-in). Those states also permit you to opt out of sharing your information with company affiliates. Federal law presently doesn't allow you to stop companies from sharing information with affiliated companies.

- **Opt out of unsolicited credit offers.**

Choose to exclude your name from credit bureau lists for unsolicited credit offers ("You've been pre-approved!"). This will limit the number of pre-approved offers of credit that you receive. These, when tossed into the garbage, are potential targets of identity thieves, who use them to order credit cards in your name.

The credit reporting agencies are required by law to provide a toll-free number that you can call to request that your name not be sold for credit solicitations. Call (888) 5OPTOUT, or (888) 567-8688. Your request is shared with all three credit bureaus.

- **Don't forget to ask companies not to share with their affiliates.**
  Unfortunately, the federal law is weak regarding sharing with affiliate companies. Federal law allows companies to share your information with affiliates without the right to opt out. Write to your banks and credit card companies (return receipt requested) and ask them to remove you from their promotional lists. Ask them not to sell your name, creditworthiness, or spending habits to any third party (or affiliate) or other company without your permission. Demand that they protect your privacy.

- **Alert your professional or trade associations not to sell your data.**
  Many professional organizations sell their member lists for marketing purposes. Write your professional associations and ask them to stop selling your name and other information to other entities.

- **Don't participate in phone surveys, marketing surveys, or contests.**
  Phone surveys and contests hook you in to gather information to sell. Also, don't fill in personal information on product war-

ranty or registration cards. Information about your income is not needed to warranty your new TV. Remember, information you provide could be used to steal your good name.

- **Notify your state's Department of Motor Vehicles that you don't want your personal data sold.**

  Illinois prisoners were data processing the personal information for vehicle licenses to save money for the state. These criminals, armed with private information, had many opportunities to commit identity theft.

  Find out how your personal information is entered into your state's databases and complain where appropriate. Ask to have your name removed from lists that are sold to marketers.

  Some states still use the Social Security number for the driver's license number. If this is the case in your state, ask for an alternative number.

- **Sign up for the Federal Trade Commission's National Do Not Call Registry:**
  (888) 382-1222 or **www.donotcall.gov**
  Stop unwanted telemarketing and pretext calling.

- **If you are called by a company you already do business with, and don't want to be called, ask them to add you to their internal database as a Do Not Call.**
  Most companies will honor that request.

- **Stop the selling of your information, which produces junk mail.**
  Contact Mail Preference Service, and sign up for the opt-out list.

  Direct Marketing Association, Mail Preference Service,
  P. O. Box 643

Carmel, NY 10512.

It is free to opt out by mail, but you are charged $5 to sign up at their web site.

Visit:

www/dmaconsumers.org/consumerassistance.html

- **Find out what the Insurance Industry Database of Property Loss Claims is selling and sharing about you.**
  You can obtain your homeowner's or automobile insurance claims history, by contacting an information broker: Choicepoint, P.O. Box 105108, Atlanta, GA 30348. Phone: (888) 497-0011. Web: **www.choicetrust.com.**

- **Don't let tax assessor records be sold with your property information**
  Contact these companies and opt out of having your information made available online for fraudsters to use.
  Acxiom: Opt-Out Hotline (877) 774-2094, or e-mail optout@acxiom.com.
  DataQuick: Opt-Out Hotline (877) 970-9171.

- **Learn what the public records show potential scammers about you.**
  Public records are documents that are open to inspection by any person. In fact, now they are easily downloadable on the Internet from myriad information brokers; many are available at no cost. Depending on your resident state, certain records may or may not be public. Normally, birth records (include your mother's maiden name), marriage certificates (your Social Security number and other personal information), death records (the decedent's Social Security numbers included in the death index), court files, divorce files (court records often have sensitive financial information and personal identifiers), arrest records (Social Security number), property ownership,

tax information, minutes of meetings of government entities, driver's license information, occupational and professional licenses, Securities and Exchange Commission filings, and governmental contracts are considered public records. Once a record becomes public, there is usually no restriction on use in the public domain. This information, available to criminally minded persons, exposes you to the risk of identity theft.

When commercial profilers buy and sell your public information for marketing and targeted advertising, they also make your data accessible to those who would use this information to commit fraud. Information brokers such as ChoicePoint and many others collect and assemble your data and then sell detailed dossiers to law enforcement, attorneys, governmental agencies, and others. It's impossible for you to know how many persons have had access to your personal information from the re-selling of that information. Additionally, these databases often contain errors, and such errors could be severe enough to falsely identify you as a criminal. Faulty records may result in a case of unintentional identity theft. Additionally, public records provide all the information necessary for an impersonator to pose as you and obtain financial records from your bank (or other private information from companies with which you do business) by practicing what is called "pretext" calling and steal money from your bank.

Two Brooklyn men allegedly usurped the identities of such luminaries as Oprah Winfrey, George Soros and Ted Turner to steal millions of dollars. Clearly no one is immune to identity theft, a range of crimes that runs from stealing credit card numbers to concocting phony personas, complete with credit reports and college degrees.

That's what the New York City Police Department's Computer Investigations and Technology Unit learned when it cracked the case of Abraham Abdallah and Michael Pugliese, the two men *arrested and charged with possession of forged instruments and attempted grand larceny. The men had allegedly obtained credit reports and other information about some of America's wealthiest individuals to access their brokerage, credit card and bank accounts using pretext calling. It was revealed after Merrill Lynch received an e-mail requesting that $10 million be transferred from the account of Thomas Siebel, founder of the software firm Siebel Systems, to an account in Australia. The transfer would have caused an "imbalance" in Siebel's account, so the brokerage firm contacted him. The executive said he never made the request. Merrill Lynch then found similar requests by phone and e-mail on the accounts of other well-known clients and alerted the authorities.*

Under present law, you have no right to opt out of having your public record information sold, shared, or transferred; nor are you notified when vast profiles are being amassed about you. You have no privacy (control over the sharing of this information) when it comes to public records. This is one of the many reasons that, even if you are able to execute all of the actions in this book, there is some information dissemination that is beyond your control. It's critical to minimize your risk where you can, but also be aware of the dangers lurking in these public records. Some states are beginning to see the vulnerability of these records and have passed laws requiring that sensitive information be redacted for the general public like the Social Security numbers of parents on birth certificates. This is a healthy approach to allowing public access without divulging riskier data. Urge your legislators to consider more protections for sensitive information in public records.

As a democracy, we value the right of access to public records and freedom of information to insure that government agencies are accountable. However, in this age of databases of personal information, we need to a balance what the public needs to know against our right to protect our personal information.

11. Protect yourself while using your computer

- **Set up a systems password to get into your computer**
  Set up a system password requirement (for your computer and laptop) before Windows even begins to load. It will prohibit any access to the computer except for the one who enters your password, which should only be you! Check your computer manual to set up the password.

- **Install firewalls**
  Hardware firewalls block all traffic between the Internet and your network that isn't explicitly allowed. A hardware firewall keeps unauthorized programs and people from remotely accessing your computer. These firewalls can also hide the addresses of the computers behind your firewall, making individual computers on your network invisible to the outside. You can purchase an inexpensive hardware router / firewall from such companies as LinkSys, Microsoft and D-Link.

  Software firewalls, such as the Microsoft Internet Connection Firewall, ZoneAlarm, and Norton Personal Firewall protect only the computer they're running on. It's a good backup defense to hardware firewalls, but software firewalls on their own cannot protect your entire network if you have several computers linked in your home.

- **Install, use, and continually update anti-virus software**
  Antivirus software screens all incoming data and files to determine whether a known virus is trying to infect your computer, then gives you a choice to delete, repair or quarantine the file. Every time you download files, receive e-mails or even put a CD or floppy on your computer, you need to scan for virus

infections. Viruses can be coded to scan your computer for financial information like your tax return, which could subject you to identity theft.

- **Don't just give your computer away when you purchase a new one.**
  Some people think deleting the files will clean them from your computer. But this information can be easily retrieved by computer techies. So instead, use an overwrite or erasing program to override the entire hard drive. Go to **www.hq.nasa.gov/office/oig/hq/harddrive.pdf** on the National Aeronautics and Space Administration web site for more information.

- **Use hard drive eraser software.**
  If you have sensitive files with your personal information on your computer or laptop, you can use a program called Erasure to erase just those files. You can use the security level you wish, and you can also remove sensitive information stored without your knowledge. Go to **www.east-tec.com** and you can find erasure software for your computer as well as for your CD's or other removable media. You can also find East-Tec Disc Sanitizer, which can securely destroy all data on any hard drive or floppy disc.

- **Don't store financial or sensitive information on your laptop.**
  In fact, if you have any personal identifying information or any financial files or confidential files that you must keep on your laptop, put it in an encrypted file. Make sure you don't use an automatic log-in feature, which displays your name and password. Always take the extra step of using a password with numbers, symbols, and letters so it would harder for the thief to get into your computer.

- **Secure your laptop while traveling on airplanes**
  Use caution when putting your laptop on the security screener in the airport. Make sure that you place your other bags first, so that you'll have time to get through the screening before someone steals your laptop.
  Once onboard your flight, stow your computer in your bag under the seat in front of you. Avoid putting it in the overhead bin where others will have easier access to it.

- **Encrypt your confidential data.**
  If you have sensitive information on your computer, encrypt it. Programs such as Pretty Good Privacy (**www.pgp.com**) make the job easy, and if you have Windows XP, you already have the tools needed. If a thief gets your machine, these extra steps will make it much more difficult to access the laptop's data.

- **Back up your data before you leave for your trip.**
  If your laptop should be stolen on your trip, you may be able to get another computer at your destination and download your important files—at least you'll have your data on CD. Don't keep the back- up file in the same computer case as your laptop.

- **Trace a stolen laptop's location.**
  If your laptop does get stolen, you can purchase a program that will report the location of a stolen laptop. These programs work when the laptop connects to the Internet. Tracing programs include zTrace (**www.ztrace.com**), CyberAngel (**www.sentryinc.com**) and ComputracePlus (**www.computrace.com**).
  Also, engraving your name on your computer will make it more difficult for the thief to sell.

- **Be on the lookout for charlatans who can access your home computer even if you are not connected to the Internet.**
  Your home is your refuge—so it's easy to forget that a crime

could be committed there without a physical burglary. If you keep identifying information and confidential data on a computer without protecting it from the view of others, you are at risk of identity fraud. Ask yourself the following questions: Who has access to my home computer? Do my children bring friends to our home to use our PC? Do I use a cleaning service? Are repairpersons or household workers entering our home? Do guests and roommates have access to our processor? Are we using a wireless connection so that several computers in our home can network?

12. Protect yourself on the Internet.

> *There's a lot of things you can do with the Internet to destroy someone from the comfort of your own home.*
>
> —Dave Gordon, Maine police officer

- **Strengthen your computer's log-in security**

Your passwords are the keys to unlock the door to your identity, guard them! Don't be lazy and store them on your computer or on the web site itself. Type them in each time you access a particular site.

Learn how to browse the Internet and send e-mail messages without leaving a trail. (See PC World at **www.pcworld.com** and other computer magazines for ideas to protect your privacy when using the Internet.)

In addition, don't give out your Internet account password to anyone. If you do, you may find unexpected charges on your bill and lots of other problems.

Here's a suggestion for effective password creation: Use the first or last letters of each word in a favorite line of poetry that you'll easily remember. Intersperse these letters with numbers and punctuation marks. Example: "Mary had a little lamb." M*HA2LL or Y!DAE9B. Upper and lower case can also be varied. M*ha2LL.

- **Don't give your password to anyone.**
  We suggest that you have at least two passwords: One password (using letters and numbers, at least eight characters long, as above) for your very sensitive and private information, and another one for your less sensitive web site entries. Make sure that you lock up your passwords in a locked drawer, cabinet, or safe. Change your passwords every six months.

- **Tell your Internet service provider that your personal data is not for sale.**
  Find out the company's privacy policy. Inform the service that any information you provide is not for sale and that you will hold the service accountable if it fails to maintain your privacy.

- **Look for and read privacy policies.**
  For every web site that asks you to register or provide information, take a minute and read their policy carefully. It should be easy for you to find and if it is not, then we advise you not to fill in any information. The policy should tell you what information they're collecting, what they're using, and how they're sharing it. You can also find out what kind of security they're using to protect your information. If you still want to do business with a company that doesn't have a privacy policy, then e-mail their web site and ask them to specifically answer you in writing what the policy is, and ask them to post one. Some states, like California, require companies to post a privacy policy.

- **Look for a privacy seal.**
  TrusTe and the Better Business Bureau provide a seal program that's backed up by that company's willingness to handle com-

plaints by consumers who feel that their privacy has been violated. This helps companies institute a system for "walking their talk" in protecting privacy. Unfortunately, a privacy seal doesn't necessarily mean that the company is not a fraud, because sometimes the bad guys can steal a privacy seal and place it on their web site, as well.

- **Don't register when visiting web sites on the Internet, unless you are certain it's not a hoax site.**
  Web page owners have the ability to collect data about you when you visit their site and store that information in "cookie" files on your computer, which they can also share with other websites. Ask web site operators what they do with your personal data before you give too much information. The more information someone can access about you, the easier it is to assume your identity.

  Watch out for fake sites that purport to offer services or sell goods, but which are nothing more than vehicles for collecting Social Security numbers and credit card account numbers for identity theft purposes. Always heed the old adage: only do business with known, reputable companies. Check out the company and make sure it has a real address and phone number.

- **Don't display your personal or family information on the Internet.**
  Think twice before creating your own homepage, family tree, or photo web site with identifying information about your family. These web sites give the imposter lots of data with which to create his or her new identity, including mothers' maiden names and dates of birth.

- **Shield your children online.**

  ➢ **Place the computer that your children will use for school**

in a family-oriented space in your house, such as the kitchen, family room, or recreation room. That way, you don't have to worry about your children in their bedroom and who they're "chatting" with.

➢ **Explain to your children the dangers of giving out personal information online. Alert your children that when they register for a newsletter or products, they should use a temporary e-mail address from Hotmail or Yahoo.**

➢ **After your child has used the computer, check the computer for downloads from e-mail or online sources.**

➢ **Remind your children never to put personal information about themselves or any information or photos of their family on the Internet.**

- **Set limits for your children.**
  Warn your children about peer-to-peer file sharing. Not only is there a problem with sharing music, parents should be concerned about getting sued for copyright infringement, but also make your kids aware that viruses and hackers use the peer-to-peer file sharing to access sensitive files on their computer.

  Also, warn your children to be careful when letting their friends use your PC. Unfortunately, computer privacy intrusions are often committed by people who have the opportunity to do it, such as friends and family members. So warn your children never to let someone else use your computer, unless they're sitting right there with them. For more information go to **www.safekids.com**.

- **Be cautious with peer-to-peer file sharing (p-2-p)**
  You may associate peer-to-peer file sharing with sharing business files, but people share all types of files. Perhaps the biggest concern with file sharing is that dangerous material can

be embedded with the downloaded files. For example, some bad viruses may be disguised as MP3 files that your teenager downloads onto your computer with music.

- **Don't trust love interests you meet online.**
  Use extreme caution when participating in chat rooms. True, you may find the love of your life, but you might also run into an evil-minded criminal. So don't give out personal information to people you do not know. Remain anonymous and use a nickname for your screen name.

- **Erase your name from Internet online directories.**
  If you're in the white pages of the phone book, you're likely to be on any number of Internet directories. Most online directories provide opt-out opportunities. Take advantage of them. Below I've listed several such directories, but there are many more.
  www.bigfoot.com
  www.Four11.com
  www.InfoSpace.com
  www.Switchboard.com
  www.whowhere.com

- **Opt out of "look-up" companies' databases.**
  Take advantage of the opt-out opportunities of the major information vendors such as Lexis-Nexis (**www.lexis-nexis.com**).

- **Opt out of the sharing of online cookie data with advertisers.**
  Network Advertising Initiative: **www.networkadvertising.org**

- **Use a secure browser that complies with the industry security standard, such as Secure Lock Standards (SSL).**
  The little lock that will appear at the bottom right-hand side of your screen will show you that the file will be encrypted or

scrambled as it goes through cyberspace. Once again, please remember that some fraudster sites also can use SSL, so you need to verify whom you are really dealing with.

- **Make purchases on the Internet only with reputable companies.**
  At a minimum, be sure that the company has a physical address, not just a post office box, and a telephone number where you can call and talk to them directly offline. Check with your state's attorney general for any adverse reports of the company you are dealing with. (This is not always an absolute guarantee, though, since your attorney general. or the FBI, is not always familiar with the new fraudulent companies that arise.) If possible, find the item you wish to purchase, then order by calling the 800 number to give your credit card by phone.

- **Make sure you are on the web site of the company that you really think you're doing business with.**
  Online fraudsters create web site names (URLs) very similar to those of legitimate companies. To check whether the site that you're on is really the legitimate company, go to **www.whois.net**, which tells you who has registered the URL and the physical address of that company.

  If the URL in the address section of that Web page doesn't exactly match the site you think it is, go to the front page of the actual site (i.e. **ebay.com**, **PayPal.com**, **Best Buy.com**, **AOL.com**) and scroll down to the billing section. Whenever you are questioning the URL site, it's best to call the customer service number on your bill or on the real web site that you have found to ask them if, indeed, the URL you are dealing with is correct.

- **Only give out information that's necessary for the transaction.**

Don't give out more information than is necessary for your purchase. For example, if you buy something with a credit card, you'll most likely be required to give your name, address, credit card number, expiration date, and perhaps the security number on the back or front of your credit card; but you should never be required to give your Social Security number, birth date, or mother's maiden name.

- **Other protections when purchasing online.**
  Check the company sales policies. Look at the delivery time, warranty information, and check the final costs, including shipping. Print this information and keep it in a locked file in case you encounter a problem later. Also, make sure that you copy down the 800 number to call in case there is a problem. (Online orders are protected under the Federal Mail / Telephone Order Merchandise Rule, which means that unless they state otherwise, the merchandise must be delivered to you within 30 days. So, mark your calendar to make sure that you receive your merchandise within 30 days.)

- **Use your credit card to order, it's safer than sending a check or cash.**
  Never send cash, because it doesn't create a record of your payment. Also, don't send a check because if the company is fraudulent, your money is gone. When you use a credit card, if you haven't received the product by the time your credit card statement arrives, you can let the credit card company know that you have not received the product, and you can dispute the charge until the merchandise arrives.

- **Consider a one-time-only credit card for shopping online**
  Consider using one-time use credit cards. Many credit card companies now offer a single-use credit card, which gives you

a unique number that links to your regular credit card number, but is only good for a few transactions. Your true credit card number is never placed online. Therefore, you can use the credit cards for a limited amount of purchases. The charges will show up on your monthly statement, but the vendor will never see your true credit card number. Go to your credit card company's web site and see if they offer this service. This will protect your real card from fraud.

- **Junk e-mail.**
  You can use your delete key to manage incoming junk mail, but it takes forever, especially if you get a hundred junk mails per day. Consider using a junk mail filter. Microsoft Outlook, Eudora for the PC, Entourage for Macintosh, AOL, and Hotmail all have junk mail filters. Get information on this and save yourself a great deal of time and also protect your identity. A great deal of junk mail is a "come-on" by fraudsters. Don't be fooled.

- **Use disposable forwarding e-mail addresses.**
  It is a good idea to create separate addresses or accounts that can be used for online purchases, chat rooms, and other public postings. You can create such e-mail addresses with Hotmail or with Yahoo that will protect your identity.

- **Protect yourself when you are "always on" the Internet, with connections like DSL and cable networks.**
  "Always on" users have permanent addresses that are easy for hackers and fraudsters to find and exploit. Make sure you use a router and firewall protection.

- **Applying for a job online.**
  If you post your résumé online, include only the most relevant personal information and keep details of your work history

to a minimum, since someone else can steal your identity and apply for the same job.

Limit the amount of information you share online with any web site. Approach every data request with a great deal of skepticism and with these questions: "Why do you need that information?" "How would that information be used?" "What happens if I don't give you that information?"

- **Look over your shoulder when online.**
  Look around to see who's watching you when you go online at work or at a friend's house or at Starbuck's. People around you can watch what you're doing. Never let anyone see you input a password on your computer. Use your hand to shield you're the keyboard so no one can see the letters that you're inputting.

- **Never use a public computer, such as an Internet café, a library, or airport computer to access your sensitive financial information.**
  Fraudsters love to access these public computers. They download key logging software or attach key logging hardware that records every key typed in and every web site accessed. You have no idea that your keystrokes are captured. When the fraudster returns (after you're gone), he accesses the hidden key log and has all the information you had input. If you typed in passwords and confidential information, he can steal your identity and transfer money out of your accounts.

- **Never buy anything from spammers.**
  People who send out these unsolicited e-mails are not to be trusted.

- **Be careful when buying from Internet auctions.**
  Make sure that the seller has a telephone number that you

can call, because you should be able to talk with the seller if you win the auction. Before you send any funds, talk with the seller. Beware that they may have only a temporary cell phone number, which they can cancel quickly. Ask questions that help you find out more about their authenticity.

- **Use a reliable pay service such as PayPal.com or escrow.com.**
  If you're shopping on eBay and other auction sites, carefully read the section of their web site that gives tips for safe purchasing. Get consumer advice when shopping online and call 1-877-FTC-HELP or visit The Federal Trade Commission at **www.FTC.gov**.

- **Complain at the FBI's web site for fraud.**
  Internet shopping is a blessing and a burden. You can get a wide variety of goods and services that you can't find locally, but at the same time, you don't really know who to trust. It's easy to be defrauded, so if you become a victim, make a complaint at the FBI web site at **www.IFCCFBI.gov**. Unfortunately, so many people are ripped off on the Internet that you probably won't get an investigation and, most certainly, you won't get your money back. However, if these fraudsters create a pattern of crimes, the FBI just might hear from enough victims so that they will investigate and find these criminals.

- **Never download any file that you don't recognize.**
  It's best to run your virus scanner over all attachments before you open them. Even with this precaution, you could become infected with a virus that literally steals information out of your files. If you receive a file that is not described in the body of the e-mail, even if it's from a good friend or trusted person, delete it. It's best to e-mail back to the person who sent you the file, and ask if indeed they sent you an attachment,

and what was in it before you download it. Beware that even the virus scanners and antivirus software can hardly keep up with the new malicious technology. There may be times when the software misses a virus and your computer could become infected.

- **Download all patches for your programs.**
  Get on an e-mail notification service (like Microsoft) so that you know to download all new patches in Windows and other programs you use. These patches will provide a defense for the vulnerabilities or holes that are in the software that the bad techies find out about.

- **Delete cookies or use anti-cookie software.**
  Web sites use cookies or little pieces of data that they place on your hard drive to keep track of your visits. These cookies tell the company you are visiting, the pages you visited, and also can keep track of what you purchase online. With companies you trust, a cookie is helpful because it saves you from having to identify yourself with the web site and the company each visit. It may often capture your user ID and password. It also can collect personal information to do market research. Even though a cookie doesn't have very much text, it provides your user ID when you visit a web site. The little data files reveal all the things that you've done on that company's web site. So, if companies surreptitiously put these cookies on your hard drive, and you're not comfortable with that, you can delete them. You can click on the cookies that you wish to delete, and keep those from companies that you regularly do business with. For example, if there's a cookie from American Express or your bank or another trusted company that you deal with, you may not want to delete it. Instead just delete those cookies from companies that you don't wish to continue to do business

with. You can also set your cookie warning level so that you can be warned before you accept or reject cookies.

- **Protect yourself from spyware.**
  Spyware programs capture information about you from your computer. These insidious programs are usually embedded into other programs that you download. Good and bad guys collect data about us when we're online. We don't even know or give our consent, so that's why this is called spyware. Deleting spyware can be very challenging. To rid your PC of spyware and pop-up adware, download free software called Spybot. You can get this at **www.download.com** at no cost. There is also Spy Cop (**www.spycop.com**), which will alert you if you're being watched or if key-logging programs are on your computer. Spyware and key-logging programs can watch you as you use online bill paying services, make deposits or review your financial statements online.

- **Rid yourself of pop-ups or adware.**
  These pop-ups are irritating and also may carry viruses. Go to **www.ada-ware.com** to download the software to eliminate them.

- **Other tips for keeping your e-mail safe and personal information out of the hands of identity thieves.**
  Minimize the information that you put in your e-mail signature file. If your e-mail is used for your business, of course you're going to want to put your contact information so people can do business with you. But you should not be putting your home address, home phone number and other personal data in your signature file.

- **Don't put your e-mail address on your web site.**
  If you put your e-mail address on your personal web site or

your business web site, you will get thousands of spam e-mails. Instead, create a contact box where visitors can fill in information and send e-mails without seeing your e-mail address. Once you have a relationship with them, then of course, they'll see the e-mail address you are using when you write back to them. Then it is your choice to provide it to them.

- **Search out your name on the Web to find what information is circulating about you.**
  Misinformation might be reported about you that could be a result of someone else using your name.

- **Don't get hooked by a "phishing" expedition.**
  "Phishing" is a scam that involves deception and identity theft. The imposters create bogus e-mails, pretending to be from reputable companies to trick victims into revealing personal information including Social Security numbers, credit card numbers, personal identifying numbers, and online banking passwords. The con is to gain the confidence of the victim and appear real, using authentic-looking logos and Web addresses (URLs) that look impressively similar to the real Web address for the company they are impersonating. In April 2004, a survey conducted by the Gartner technology research firm estimated that 52 million American adults had received phishing e-mails within the past year. Of those surveyed who received such e-mails, 3 percent, (representing about 1.8 million individuals), said they disclosed personal or financial information. Gartner concluded that at least another million have unwittingly fallen for phishing lures—don't you be one of those who gets hooked.

  Here's an example of an alarming authentic-looking "phishing" expedition that pretends to be from Wells Fargo Bank:

Dear Wells Fargo Account Holder,

We regret to inform you, that we had to block your Wells Fargo account because we have been notified that your account may have been compromised by outside parties. Our terms and conditions you agreed to state that your account must always be under your control or those you designate at all times. We have noticed some activity related to your account that indicates that other parties may have access and or control of your information in your account. These parties have in the past been involved with money laundering, illegal drugs, terrorism and various Federal Title 18 violations. In order that you may access your account we must verify your identity by clicking on the link below. Please be aware that until we can verify your identity no further access to your account will be allowed and we will have no other liability for your account or any transactions that may have occurred as a result of your failure to reactivate your account as instructed below. Thank you for your time and consideration in this matter. Please follow the link below and renew your account information.

https://online.wellsfargo.com/cgi-bin/signon.cgi

Before you reactivate your account, all payments have been frozen, and you will not be able to use your account in any way until we have verified your identity.

This authentic looking scam caught many people. Are you guarding yourself from getting hooked by a hoax like the sample above? Here are some safeguards:

- **Never answer any e-mail that asks either directly, indirectly, or through a web site for your personal or financial identifying information.**
  If you are told that you need to update your information online, don't update it. Don't click on the web site in the e-mail.

Instead, go to the Web address that you know and write an e-mail asking if there is any account maintenance needed on your account. Or call the 800 number that's listed on the true Web page. Make a copy of the questionable web site's URL and forward it to the legitimate business and ask if the request is legitimate.

- **Don't ever respond or reply to the "phishing" e-mail or the fraudster will have your real e-mail address, and perhaps your contact information that you include with your signature.**
- **Don't be gullible.**
  There are many hoaxes and scams and outright lies on the Internet. You don't know who you're dealing with or where they are located. If you are like most honest people, you are eager to help someone in need. Unfortunately, the Internet is filled with requests for help and sympathy letters asking for donations for Make-A-Wish, The Diabetes Foundation, American Cancer Society, etc. If you want to make a donation to one of the legitimate charities, call the nonprofit organization that you'll find listed in your yellow pages and make a donation to a legitimate company with a verifiable address.
- **Be cautious of scam letters.**
  One such hoax is the Nigerian scam letter. The FBI reports that millions of scammed investors have responded to various Nigerian scam letters. You may have received an e-mail asking for your help, explaining that hundreds of thousands of dollars are currently stashed in a foreign country. The scammer contacts you and asks that you allow the money to be transferred to a bank account in your name and then you get a portion of the funds. At least 17 people have been killed because they have fallen for the Nigerian scam, and in their quest for money

have actually met the fraudsters. If you lose money to a scam, you will never retrieve it, and you may lose more than your identity; you may lose your life.

To find out about more of these financial scams, go to the United States Secret Service web site at **www.secretservice.gov.** If you receive any of these letters, forward them on to the Secret Service, the FBI, or the Federal Trade Commission, but do not ever reply to the sender. (See our resources list in Chapter Eight.) Forward this and other types of spam to Spam@uce.gov.

- **Don't put confidential or controversial information in your e-mail.**
  Your e-mail is like a postcard; so before you write any information in an e-mail to a friend, colleague, or family member, ask yourself if you would display this information on a poster board for anyone else to see. If you wouldn't want other people to see this e-mail, don't send it. If you want to send confidential information in an e-mail, then your best bet is to use encryption software to protect it. (i.e., **www.pgp.com**)

- **Be cautious when participating in instant messaging.**
  Often people think because they're sitting in the privacy of their own kitchen, bedroom, or office that their IM conversations with a friend are confidential. First, ask yourself is this person really a friend? Have you ever met this person? Is the person that you think you're talking to really who he says he is? Don't trust any stranger online, and if you are corresponding with a good friend, don't share secrets online.

- **Take extra precautions to hide on the Internet**
  Remember not to reveal your gender, age, where you live, or anything personal about yourself when posting messages online.

- **Sign up for e-mails that are disposable.**
  If you get a temporary e-mail address at Hotmail, Yahoo or Google, then after awhile if you're not comfortable or you feel that you're being harassed, or your identity is in danger, you can close that account. Also, this will help you to reduce the spam that you receive from giving that e-mail out on list servers, posting boards, etc.

- **Re-read your e-mail several times before sending.**
  In our haste to write e-mail (because it is such a simple means of communication), we may often send out more information than we need to. So take your time and re-read your e-mail before you push the Send button. Once it's in cyberspace, you can't retrieve it.

- **Visit an Internet safety organization such as Cyber Angels (www.cyberangels.org) or the Federal Trade Commission (www.FTC.gov), for additional precautions.**
  New scams are created each day, and we can't list them all. The bottom line is, just be skeptical of everything online.

- **Don't fall in love too quickly with online matchmaking.**
  Cyber dating and matchmaking services are very popular these days. But your cyber date may be impersonating another person or even lying about everything from age to gender to career, etc. So ask yourself these questions when communicating with a potential love relationship online: How much information do I really want to give out? Is this person in too much of a hurry to meet me? Is he or she wanting to become intimate too fast or asking too many personal questions before we get to know each other? Have I done a Web search with this person's name on the Internet to find out who he or she really is? If you set up a time to meet this person, will it be for lunch or coffee in a public place? Use your own transportation so that you can leave

immediately if you are uncomfortable. Let friends and family know that you are going to meet someone so if there is a problem, they can reach you or you can reach them by cell phone.

- **Anonymous Internet connection.**
  Normally, when you're connected to the Internet, you're transactions are visible to various ISP servers. If you wish to surf the net anonymously, then shield yourself from Web bugs, viruses, cookies, and others. You may wish to use Anonymiser software. Go to **www.anonymiser.com**

Now that you have taken an inventory of what tasks you need to perform to protect your personal information, and limit your susceptibility to identity theft, you're probably feeling that it's an intimidating mission. Remember, information is potential power, and you now have the knowledge and ability to use these valuable tools to Safeguard Your Identity. To ease your mind, just start with these three easy and important steps:

- **Order your credit reports at least twice a year.**
- **Shred your personal and confidential information before discarding it.**
- **Don't trust anyone on the Internet.**
  These three steps will set you on a positive course to initiate your personal privacy protection plan. You've now identified what you already do to protect your personal privacy and what steps you wish to put into action in the future. In Chapter Three, you'll learn to assess how well you are protecting your identity while outside your home.

Chapter Three

It's a Jungle Out There: Safekeeping Your Identity Outside of Your Home

Honesty pays, but it don't seem to pay enough to suit some people.

—Kin Hubbard (1868 - 1930), US journalist, humorist, homespun philosopher.

Dave, a law enforcement officer, and his wife completed a loan application to refinance their home. He diligently completed all sections including his Social Security number, his wife's Social Security number, all of his bank account numbers, the balance in his accounts, all of his credit card accounts, etc. Indeed, his whole financial profile and that of his wife were completely disclosed. Several months later, he began receiving phone calls, letters, and demands for payment for the numerous new accounts that had been opened in his name with credit card companies with whom he had never dealt. Dave soon learned, after his own extensive investigation, that he and several other innocent homeowners who had refinanced their homes had become victims of an insider who had access to those loan applications. Apparently, a now ex-employee had made copies of the loan applications, sold them to his friends, who proceeded to assume the identity of numerous couples who trusted the lender to secure and protect their information.

Your daily activities require you to share numerous bits and pieces of your personal information. Although much of what happens with that information once you divulge it to others is beyond your control, you can take the time to ask questions and demand privacy protection for your information. And you should know that if a company mishandles your information, is negligent with it, provides access to it to those who could hurt you, you may have legal remedies.

Remember, a little paranoia with regard to protecting your identity isn't such a bad idea. Being conscious of the ways in which you may be vulnerable, will make you much more aware of what could happen to you every time you share sensitive personal information. Quiz businesses, agencies, and professionals with whom you deal and make them more aware so that they'll be more cautious, as well. The following suggested steps will help you guard yourself in the outside world. If you do these things already, check them off and feel proud! If you don't, consider adding these action items into your daily activities.

Protect Yourself When Completing Applications

When filling out applications to buy or refinance a home or lease a car, to obtain an equity line of credit, open a college or investment account, or purchase stock, etc., ask yourself the following questions:

- Have you investigated the company to make sure that it is truly reputable? (You may wish to check the Better Business Bureau for complaints.)
- Did a trusted friend, colleague, or government agency refer you to this company?
- Have you completed only the information that was absolutely necessary for the application?
- Have you expressed your concern about identity theft and asked how the information would be stored and secured? (i.e. Are forms encrypted online? Are there laptops that are transported outside of the business office? Are there locked cabinets? Who would access them? How would access be limited? Where will the information be held once the loan is approved or rejected? Will the original application be returned to you if it is rejected? What will happen to the application if it is accepted?)
- Have you written a note at the bottom of the application or given a separate note or letter (ask for an initialed copy) that states something to this effect:

  I'm providing this sensitive data about myself and my family with assurances from this company that this data will be protected and only those who need to know this information will have access to this information. It shall not be used for any other purpose except for the purpose of this application.

  We suggest you sign the note, and have it initialed by the person who receives the application. By providing this note, you're letting the company that you're dealing with know that they are on notice that they are to protect your sensitive information. Although you may think that protecting your data should be the standard in the business world, if that were true, we would have millions fewer victims of identity theft.

Defend Yourself When Traveling

Whenever you leave the sanctity of your home, whether traveling on business or for pleasure, or just to the supermarket, be alert for ways in which people can take advantage of you to literally steal your identity.

- **Never leave your purse, wallet, or identification in your car even if it's locked.**
  Anything left behind on a car seat is an invitation for a potential fraudster to break a window and steal your items. If you have to leave something in the car, then remove your identification documents and take them with you. If you're going swimming, for example, buy one of the plastic airtight, secure document and key holders to wear around your neck like the surfers do. You can put credit cards, cash, information, and documents in it. The rest of the items you should just leave in your trunk.

- **It's better to use traveler's checks or credit cards when traveling, rather than using your checks.**
  In Chapter Two we talked about the danger of using checks and ATM cards. We suggest that you use your ATM card only for taking out cash when traveling in any country, but make sure that you don't use an ATM debit card that has a Visa / MasterCard logo on it, because if that's stolen, it can be used to take the money directly out of your account. The credit card can be easily replaced while on vacation, whereas the cash that is siphoned out of your account with an ATM debit card or by using checks is not quickly replaced, especially if you are out of the country.

- **Remove unnecessary documents and extra credit cards from your wallet before traveling.**
  Although it's a good idea to have at least two credit cards with you when traveling, just in case one is used fraudulently, it's not a good idea to bring excess cards and documents in your wallet when traveling by plane, train, or just walking down the street, especially in a foreign country. Keep a list of what items you do have in your wallet. Don't include account numbers on that list but just a telephone number and names of the companies in case you need to contact them. Pickpockets often travel to exotic locations to find unsuspecting, innocent vacationers who are distracted by family, friends and mai tai's.

- **Business Travelers Beware.**
  Secure your data when you carry a briefcase, PDA, laptop, cell phone, and other technology and equipment with sensitive information. If you travel for business, make sure that the personal and private information on your laptop (if it's absolutely necessary to carry that data on your hard drive) is password protected and contained in encrypted files.

  Also, be careful what you leave in your hotel room. Some people think that if they're in a hotel room and they have documents and sensitive equipment with personal information locked in their suitcase, that they'll be safe. However, we've heard of many victims who have had their suitcases stolen from their hotel rooms. It's best to utilize the hotel safe while you're out of the room or take the highly sensitive documents with you. Some business traveler's keep the confidential information that they have on the computer on CD's and then it's easier to lock the CDs in the safe than it is an entire laptop, since the safes often are not large enough to store larger items.

- **Carry photocopies of your sensitive information.**

Carry copies of information in your carry-on bag, so that if your wallet or briefcase is stolen, you'll have copies of all of your information to get a new passport or new credit cards. You'll also have the telephone numbers of your credit card companies.

- **Watch out for "shoulder surfers"**
  When sitting on a bus, plane, train, or other public transportation, watch out for people looking over your shoulder. Business travelers, especially, are less than cautious when using their laptops, PDAs, and other equipment that has sensitive information. This can prove especially dangerous when the business traveler gets up to use the restroom on an airplane or train and leaves his briefcases sitting next to a potential identity thief. Shoulder surfers can also take pictures with their cell phone camera or listen in on your cell phone conversations while you're waiting at the airport, or a train station. So, it's important to be aware of what you might be sharing in an oblivious manner in a public place.

- **Secure your briefcases, purses, laptops, etc. in restaurants, bars, theaters, concerts, stadiums, and other tourist areas.**
  Good-minded, honest people like you would never think of stealing someone's purse underneath a table at a fine restaurant, or stealing a briefcase from someone sitting in a waiting room for a meeting. That's why scammers target professional, innocent-looking people.

John was on his way to an important business meeting and stopped for gas. As he got out of the car to begin filling his tank, a well-dressed man walked over and asked for directions to a nearby location. John courteously offered all the help he could. When he got back in his car, he saw that his briefcase with his wallet and all of his sensitive documents for the upcoming meeting had been stolen. The professional-looking man's accomplice had grabbed it right through the open car door while John was distracted.

- **Exercise caution when someone tries to distract you.** Make sure you know where your briefcase, purse, or wallet are at all times, and if you do get out of the car or open a car door, make sure there is nothing out of your visual presence or out of touch that a fraudster could steal.
- **Don't stop your mail when you're going out of town.** Unfortunately, the post office, like most other big operations, has dirty employees. Not only have we heard of many victims who've had their mail stolen from post office boxes (and Mailboxes Etc.–type places, which are not the post office), but also numerous victims have contacted us to say that they thought the safest thing to do was to stop their mail when they left for vacation. Instead, it is far safer to get a trusted family member or, a very trusted neighbor that you've known for a long time, and have that neighbor get your mail when they pick up their own, and bring it into their house. Give them a box or a bag to leave in a locked closet in their home. You'll pick up the mail when you return from vacation.
- **Don't stop delivery of your newspaper, either.** Obviously, you don't want to have a pile of papers thrown on your doorstep. However, police tell us that insiders working for newspapers will let the bad guys know when you've gone on vacation. We suggest that you either have that trusted neighbor pick up your newspaper every morning when he picks up his, or cancel the account for your newspaper. You can always restart the account, and probably get a better rate.

- **Use caution when having neighbors and relatives come into your home while you're on vacation.**
  Although you might be eager to trust them with watering your plants and feeding and walking your dog, it's not a good idea to leave out (and within reach) sensitive information: Opened envelopes with bank statements, credit card statements, and a computer with sensitive files that's not password protected are too tempting for some people. Lock up any documents with account numbers or Social Security numbers, and don't leave cash, jewelry or credit cards around.

- **Make sure if you travel extensively and let people into your home, that you get a floor safe or locked cabinets or locking closets to make sure that you don't make it too tempting for people who come into your house to get access to your sensitive information.**

- **When traveling, use your cell phone for calls you need to make while sitting in the airport, the train station, or while in other public places.**
  If you intend to use a credit card or calling card at a public phone, consider buying a prepaid calling card. That way, the crooks can't watch you from a distance and with their mini-binoculars steal your credit card number as you enter it on the keypad. We've heard from many victims who come home after traveling and find that hundreds or thousands of dollars were charged to their credit card or their phone card before they even realized what happened.

- **Guard your bags in public restrooms.**
  All of us feel vulnerable when using a public bathroom, just hanging purses or suitcases on the hook on the door. Keep the briefcase, laptop, or whatever items you have in there close to you, and hold onto the handles so that if someone reaches

underneath the stall or attempts to grab items from the hook, they can't just grab it and run. They'll look for someone who's "easier pickings" to quickly target.

- **Be careful who you talk to when meeting strangers while traveling.**
  Con men and women are often charming and engaging. Especially when you're traveling alone; you might find yourself more easily fooled by that interesting conversationalist.

- **Be very discreet when sharing information about your travel plans.**
  Tell your employees, your travel agent, neighbors, and others that you don't want them to say that you're on vacation. It's best for your assistants and colleagues to just say that you're out of the office or not available at that time, and not to give details of your travel plans. It's a good idea not to reveal documents about your travel in public for others to see. Demand that your hotel and car rental companies not reveal personal information about you or your whereabouts. Tell them that they should not discuss anything about you or your information with anyone without a security confirmation number or code. Con men and women utilize pretext calling to find out more information about you. For example, if someone finds your hotel bill, he or she can call and pretend to be you. They can ask for certain information like: "What credit card did I use and what number was that?" So, by clarifying your concern with each of these companies, you can better protect your personal information.

Sally and George were celebrating their 30th wedding anniversary on a beautiful cruise ship. They met another couple who ate dinner with them each evening. After sharing quite a bit of information with each other, they exchanged phone numbers and addresses.

Several months later, the charming couple appeared unannounced one evening at Sally and George's door. They welcomed the couple into their home, and to their detriment were robbed at gun point of jewelry, credit cards, wallets, and identifying information. Not only were they physically assaulted, but their identity was later used, as well, for financial rape.

Although we talk about identity theft as a faceless crime, under certain circumstances brazen scammers will meet you and, not only steal from you physically (and perhaps physically harm you), but they can also rob your identity long after they're gone. Unfortunately, in our society you need to have some healthy, realistic caution. Don't trust people you meet online and don't trust people you meet offline either. Your life and identity may depend on it.

Guard Your Information in Public Places

- **Carry as little personal identifying information as possible in your wallet.**
  For starters, don't carry your Social Security card. You already know the number by now and you can take the original with you if you know you're going to be required to show it. Get rid of extra credit cards and other identifying data. In short, don't carry anything that you don't use or need.

- **Don't carry healthcare cards, employee cards or other documents that display your Social Security number.**
  As I mentioned earlier in the book, instead of carrying these cards with you, make copies of them, black out (redact) all but the last four digits of your Social Security number and place the copies back in your wallet. If you are injured in an accident, the card with your name and the last four digits will suffice to provide you the services you need.

- **Reduce the likelihood of your wallet or purse being stolen.** When in crowds, wear a fanny pack, keep your wallet in a front pocket, or keep your purse in front of you. You may prefer to keep your wallet in a pocket with a Velcro™ enclosure or put rubber bands around it so it won't slip out of your pocket so easily. Make copies of all the important cards and documents you carry and keep them in a locked cabinet at home.

- **Resist allowing your Social Security number to be used for any kind of identification, especially on your driver's license.**
  Unfortunately, too many companies, government agencies, and organizations use Social Security numbers in careless ways—as student ID numbers, for company identification badges, and on Little League rosters. It'll take courage to resist these practices. Ask to use an alternative number for identification or enrollment. Of course, you will have to provide your Social Security number to anyone who employs you, the IRS, your accountant, your bank, your investments broker, or if you are applying for a loan. But you are not required to give it to others. Unfortunately, there is no law that prohibits a company from asking for your Social Security number, so you will need to be assertive in explaining your concerns. You may be denied service for refusing to provide that number, but we suggest informing the company about the risk of identity theft. Some states are passing legislation to limit the display of Social Security numbers. (California's Confidentiality of Social Security Numbers: California Civil Code Sections 1798.85 and 1786.60.) Please visit the California Office of Privacy Protection's Recommended Practices for the display of social security numbers at **http://www.privacy.ca.gov/recommendations/Social Security numberrecommendations.pdf.** Federal legislation is also addressing this issue.

- **Don't put your address or license plate number on your key ring.**
  Doing so will merely point a thief to your home and car. If your keys have been stolen or lost and there is a way for a thief to find you, remember to change the locks on your house and automobile. Hide your car registration in a safe place in your car since it has your home address.
- **Watch out for photo cell phones and mini-video cameras.**
  When you use ATMs or display your credit card or personal information at a retail store, a sneaky criminal can capture your information on camera, so guard your information and be vigilant.

Protect Your Privacy and Identity When Dealing With Professionals

You are required to trust your doctor, dentist, tax preparer, lawyer, and other professionals with your personal, confidential, and sensitive financial information. Have you verified that they are who they say they are? Have you looked into the information-handling procedures they use in their office? Do you know who else has access to that confidential information? What are they doing to safeguard your information so that others who don't have a right to see it, have limited access? What do they do with information that they've copied and they're discarding? These are the types of questions that you need to be asking when you meet with these trusted individuals.

Jane was discussing some dental procedures including cost issues and dental insurance with her dentist in the front office, when she saw the receptionist pull her file from an unlocked cubby behind the desk. In that file, she saw her whole profile, plus an intake sheet that included Jane's Social Security number, date of birth, mother's maiden name, age, health issues, etc. Not only did the receptionist have access to these files, but many other employees and several dentists were also pulling these files. Then she realized there were files sitting out on tables in the open area near the various dental chairs. When she asked about the security of these files, the receptionist looked offended and answered, "None of us are crooks here." Jane then asked her if there was a cleaning service that came in the evening and if the building had hired the cleaning crew or if the dental corporation had hired the cleaning crew. The receptionist didn't know. Jane then attempted to talk to her dentist about the security issues with regard to her personal information and other items, and she questioned why she had to give her Social Security number when her dental insurance carrier used an alternate number. The dentist agreed to black out the last five numbers of her Social Security number and remove her mother's maiden name. But he told her: "It would be too expensive to install locked cabinets." Jane, whose sister had become a victim of identity theft, decided to get a new dentist.

- **Don't provide more information than is absolutely necessary to those from whom you seek professional services from.**
  Many health insurance companies, although they have used the Social Security number as the identification number in the past, are now willing, or are being forced, (California law and possibly pending federal law) to change the number to an alternative number. So, your healthcare professionals, unless they have a very good reason, shouldn't be collecting your Social Security number, your mother's maiden name, or your driver's license number. You're not advised to get into an argument with your service providers; however, you can gently explain to them your

concerns about sensitive information getting into the wrong hands and the epidemic of identity theft. Former victims of identity theft tell us that sensitivity is growing among businesses. Explain to your provider that your biggest concern isn't how the professional might use the information, but how others might use it to hurt you, and the provider himself.

- **Be cautious when choosing a trusted professional.** Unfortunately, doctors, lawyers, and accountants also get their identities stolen. In fact, I had my identity stolen by an imposter who then paraded herself as an attorney with business cards pretending to be me, Mari Frank, Esq. So,when hiring a legal professional in your state, call the state bar and find out as much as you can about the attorney before you hire her. Find out the address where that lawyer's business is located. You may even be able to find out his / her age and when he / she began practicing law. For doctors and dentists, you can call the state board of medical examiners or state board of dental examiners to find out if the persons that you are dealing with really are who they say they are. Your State Department of Consumer Affairs can probably advise you as to other professions and how to verify their information. You can find out if the general contractor that you have hired is really licensed and if he is truly who he says he is. Also, you can find out about any complaints against him. So, be a savvy consumer when it comes to choosing a professional to trust.

Guard Your Information That's Available to the Public

- **Protecting Your Confidential and Sensitive Medical Information**
  The Federal Health Insurance Portability and Accountability Act

(HIPAA), which became effective in April 2003, was supposed to set a higher standard for privacy protection for everyone's medical information. (For a very good explanation of your basic rights with HIPAA, visit **www.privacyrights.org** and look at fact sheet 8 and 8A.) Unfortunately, we find a great deal of identity theft information is stolen from hospitals, urgent-care units, emergency care units, doctors' offices, out-patient surgical units, and other healthcare facilities. Information also may be stolen from insurance companies, government agencies, as well as by unscrupulous employees. Although HIPPA does provide some protection for your sensitive personal and medical information, it really does not completely limit access to your information. You'll find that the waiver forms that you're asked to sign are often very confusing and general. Basically, you give your physician or other healthcare provider a blanket waiver to share your sensitive information with whomever they wish. Please note that your healthcare provider will need to share information with your healthcare insurance provider if you're applying for health insurance or you want reimbursement for healthcare services. You'll need to share information with governmental agencies that handle programs like Medi-Cal, Medicare, and worker's compensation. Also, if you file a lawsuit for personal injury, worker's compensation, or in any case in which your medical condition is an issue, opposing counsel can subpoena the relevant parts of your medical record, and it may be introduced in a public courtroom. When you apply for life insurance or health insurance, you'll be asked sensitive information including your personal and health information. Unfortunately, you are not in control of those who may have access to this information.

- **Get a copy of your medical information to see if an identity clone has become you in order to get healthcare services.**

There is a Medical Information Bureau that has an essential database of medical information that is shared by various insurance companies to review your medical history to see if they want to offer you health, life, or disability insurance. Not everybody in America has a file, but if you want to see if there is a file on you, you can write to the Medical Information Bureau, P.O. Box 105, Essex Station, Boston MA 02112, or contact on the web: **www.mib.com**. Obtaining a copy of your record will cost nine dollars.

Dr. Thompson had trouble getting approved for life insurance until he found out that his imposter had been reported with heart disease. The real Dr. Thompson was 35 and in perfect health.

With the information in your medical records, someone can impersonate you and obtain healthcare services. You'll want to limit access as much as you can to your medical records, not only for your personal privacy, but also to avoid someone using your healthcare records to assume your identity.

- **Ask your doctor or healthcare provider to be very careful when photocopying or faxing your medical records for insurance carriers or other medical providers.** Question your provider about how they're discarding extra copies and faxes, and what they're doing to maintain your confidentiality with these records.

- **Speak to your doctor about how he or she is discussing your personal health information where others can hear.** Is he speaking about your personal medical information on a cordless phone? Is he discussing this information near the lobby where others can hear, or in front of employees who have no need to know?

- **Don't participate in healthcare screenings and surveys just so you can get a free massage at a chiropractor.**
- **Don't participate in chat rooms about healthcare issues.**
- **Be very careful when sharing information on health-related web sites.**
- **When you are asked to sign a waiver by your dentist, hospital, physician, or other medical provider, ask questions and clarify everything before you sign.**
- **Make sure you consider how you want your information to be shared, and let your medical provider know your preference—in writing.**
  Read the privacy policy at your healthcare provider's office. Typically, limit the release of your information for a certain period of time and to specific healthcare providers. Make sure to include that you want your spouse, significant other, or children to have access to the information in the event that you become unable to speak for yourself with regard to your own healthcare. Update your waiver for release of your medical records, if your spouse dies, if you get a divorce, or if there is some other change in your status.
- **Specifically state that you do not want your information shared for marketing of any kind.**
  You can also add a note that you have been assured that your healthcare provider will institute proper information handling practices so that only those who have a need to know this information will receive it, and that it will be discarded in a manner that completely destroys that information.

Dealing With Attorneys and the Courts

When do you need a lawyer? Most people wish to hire a lawyer when they have a dispute that they can't resolve themselves, or if there is a matter where they need a legal representative. It's a good idea to get a legal consultation for personal injury cases, business disputes, divorce, will contests, negligence cases, breach of contract, criminal defense, etc. Most attorneys will immediately ask you for identifying information including your Social Security number, your driver's license number, and other personal information. In some cases, they are required to get this information upfront. For example, in a divorce case they must file identification documentation for child support purposes, or in bankruptcy they must verify your Social Security number. They are also going to want to verify who you are if they need to get your medical records. Just as with any other business, you need to ask your lawyer's office about how they're going to safeguard that information, who will see it, if it will be stored electronically in an encrypted file, and about all the safety precautions, so that you know how they are protecting your identity.

Even if your lawyer secures all of your personal and financial information in her office, what happens when you file a lawsuit? The filing of a lawsuit becomes public record. This means that this information can be obtained from a variety of sources including the courthouse, and in some states, quite a bit of this information can be accessed online from the courts. And, worse yet, even if it can't be accessed instantaneously online from the courts, shoddy information brokers research the files and then display it on the Internet and sell it to anyone who will pay! What can you do to prevent this from happening? Consider these thoughts when you are in need of legal help:

Is this dispute a legal issue or is it a conflict that perhaps can be resolved by negotiation or mediation?

Business disputes, labor-to-labor conflict, workplace issues, marital dissolution, and estate arguments often don't have to be resolved in the courtroom. In fact, if you file a lawsuit as an employee, knowing that this becomes public record, it may preclude you from getting a job in the future if another company thinks that you're going to be litigious, (i.e. worker's compensation, sexual harassment, or wrongful termination.) So, whenever possible, try to resolve the dispute outside of the court system. Consider using a third-party attorney / mediator who's trained in the law to help define the issues and create a problem-solving approach so that all parties retain their privacy and arrive at a mutually satisfying settlement. When accord is reached, the mediator prepares a settlement agreement that is <u>not</u> filed with the court, so the conflict remains confidential, and the agreement is a private document. Obviously, the fact that it becomes a contract means it is enforceable by a court, but normally, since the parties have settled out of court, they wish to keep the dispute and all the sensitive issues defining the dispute confidential. There is much more likelihood that the parties will follow through with their promises as a result of a mediated agreement since the parties retained control over their decision to settle.

If you are getting a divorce, you must file the essential documents with the court in order to obtain a legal marital dissolution.

This does not mean that you must divulge all your financial and sensitive information for the public to see. In fact, astute high profile people and celebrities do everything that they can to keep their "dirty laundry" and finances out of the courts. They usually agree to settle upfront, either by using attorneys who agree to not force the issue to litigation or by using a qualified attorney / mediator.

Although both parties must file the specific court forms dealing with child and spousal support (alimony in some states) and the divorce decree, it is not necessary for them to list all of their marital property in the court documents. In divorce mediation, or in collaboration, the parties will protect their privacy, their identity, and their specific financial identifiers by entering into a confidential marital settlement agreement. Although divorcing spouses have a fiduciary duty to disclose all financial documents to each other, they don't have a duty to disclose everything to the court and to the general public. The mediation process secures secrets, and financial data (such as the tax returns and financial statements) by keeping this information out of their court files.

In mediation or private arbitration, disputants avoid depositions and discovery that would be used in a trial setting. The parties still must fully disclose, but under confidential procedures. Upon settlement, sensitive information is kept out of the court files and out of the public records.

If you must file a lawsuit for any reason:

- Tell your attorney about your privacy and identity theft concerns.

- Ask your lawyer what it will take to keep the information in the case as confidential as possible. Ask him how your financial information and personal information can be kept out of the court records. Find out what he or she will do to protect certain confidential documents such as credit reports, medical records, financial statements, tax returns, etc and secure them from the court records.

- Settle the case as quickly as possible and get an agreement from all of the parties that instead of entering a stipulated judgment, you will resolve the case with a confidential settlement agreement and dismiss the underlying case with prejudice so that it may not be brought back again.

Remember, by participating in a lawsuit, you voluntarily submit yourself to the court's jurisdiction and you'll have to provide personally identifying information such as addresses, telephone numbers, birthdays, financial documents, and numerous other pieces of information about you that are quite sensitive, and that often don't even have any bearing on the merits of the case. So, in addition to exposing you to identity theft, making your personal data public information could embarrass you, could damage your business reputation, limit your future business opportunities, and expose you to other crimes. Whenever possible, avoid the public court system.

Most litigants are unaware that information that's filed is publicly accessible. Sometimes they find out how public it really is when they see it in the media, on television or in print. That information can be used and purchased by almost anyone for marketing purposes, employment background checks, for business dealings, and by shameless information brokers who sell it to identity thieves. So if you want to protect your identity, find other ways to resolve your disputes outside of the court system, because right now that information is readily available to those who could use that information to impersonate you.

Protect Your Information When Dealing With Retailers

- **Don't provide unnecessary information to retailers.** When you're shopping at the mall or online, you'll find that merchants ask for far more information than they need. For example: When you're shopping in a mall and you're paying cash, why do you have to give your address, phone number, and other identifying information? Ask the retailer what he or she plans to do with that. If the store plans to send you postcards about future sales, you may wish to allow them to take that information. However, be sure to tell them that they may not use that information to sell or share with marketers and other stores.

- **Don't provide any personal information when you're using a credit card.**
  Some people write on the back of their credit "see photo ID" instead of a signature. This forces retailers to check for a driver's license. You may show your driver's license, but don't allow retailers to write down the number anywhere (on your credit card receipt), and don't provide your Social Security number or other personal information.

- **Be aware of video recording devices, and audio recording devices in places of business, including retail stores, hotels, and offices... and look around for these devices.**
  Make sure that your personal information isn't being audio recorded and that your financial information is not being videotaped.

- **Don't share personal information about yourself to the salesclerk or storeowner.**
  Be careful when other customers are listening in or viewing what you're doing with credit cards, checks, and personal information while they're standing behind you or to the side of you in line waiting for service.

- **Be aware of your vulnerability when you're walking to**

the parking lot and putting shopping bags in the trunk of your car.
It's best to have a shopping companion to help you watch for thieves and fraudsters, and also to carry a loud whistle.

In Chapters Two and Three you have focused on how to protect yourself at home and in the outside world as an individual. In Chapter Four we'll show you how to keep your identity safe as an employee, manager, business owner, consumer and citizen. Whether you work as an owner, employee, independent contractor, homemaker or are retired, your awareness of precautions you can take to shield your privacy will reduce your risk of becoming a victim of this growing crime.

Chapter Four

From 9 to 5: Identity Theft Precautions in the Workplace

"The crime of identity theft undermines the basic trust on which our economy depends. When a person takes out an insurance policy, or makes an online purchase, or opens a savings account, he or she must have confidence that personal financial information will be protected and treated with care. Identity theft harms not only its direct victims, but also many businesses and customers whose confidence is shaken. Like other forms of stealing, identity theft leaves the victim poor and feeling terribly violated."

— President George W. Bush, 2004

The workplace is a goldmine for identity thieves; there are ample opportunities to steal personal information and databases on customers, employees, and even the business itself. Corporations and business owners need to protect the privacy and identity of themselves, their businesses, the people who work for them, their vendors, and their customers. So whether you are an employer, employee, or a customer, it pays to be aware of how to take responsibility for protecting your private information in commerce, and minimize your risk of identity theft. In this chapter I'll address the issue of privacy and identity theft protection on two levels: first from within the business—how to protect the employees, vendors, contractors, and owners; and second from outside—how to provide safe procedures for your customers and clients. Use the suggestions in this chapter as a workplace audit to examine your present experiences in commerce, and help you create a successful precautionary strategy.

Protection for Job Seekers

Job seekers are vulnerable to identity theft in many ways, since ads online or offline require them to provide very personal information, including Social Security numbers. One client's victimization kept him from getting a job for years.

David was laid off from a position in the healthcare industry. He had an excellent performance evaluation and felt certain that although he was laid off, he'd be able to find a new job in a short period of time. Months went by and, although David was granted interviews, he was always denied the position after authorizing a background check. After a year of numerous rejections, he hired a private investigator to help him learn why he couldn't secure a position. His credit reports were fine, but his criminal background check revealed three DUI convictions, as well as an arrest for murder on his record. He was shocked to see this, and suddenly understood the problem. Not one potential employer had told him that he was denied the position because of the criminal background check. This profile was not David's history. He had never been stopped for speeding, let alone for driving under the influence, and certainly had never been arrested for murder. Only after David's story was shown on Dateline was he able to secure employment by sending copies of the Dateline segment to each and every potential employer with a cover letter explaining what had happened to him. Even after David cleared his record with law enforcement, careless information brokers on the Internet kept reselling the erroneous information until David finally filed a lawsuit and settled. The false information will never completely be erased from databases—but David now explains his situation before authorizing any background check.

The moral of the story is: Always conduct your own background check before you allow an employer to do one.

Here are some other tips:

- **When completing an application for a job, don't provide your Social Security number until you are strongly considered for a position.**
  At that time, you will probably be required to give your Social Security number so the company can access your credit report. They'll also need your Social Security number in order to perform a background check. You'll need to provide your written permission for them to either pull your credit report or do a background check. If you are concerned about a problem in your past, let the company know about it upfront, prior to allowing them to see your credit report or your criminal background check. That way, you'll have the chance to explain any issue.

- **Before you apply for a position, review your own credit report completely.**
  Most negative items or derogatory information is legally allowed to stay on your credit report for seven years. Bankruptcies, however, will remain on your credit report for 10 years. Make sure that your credit report is accurate. It's best, if possible, to pay your bills up to date so that when the potential employer pulls your credit report, it will be exemplary. Although you

may believe that your credit report has nothing to do with your job, many employers feel that if you can't manage your finances, you might be a risk for theft, especially if you're dealing with financial information. Many employers may believe that if you need money, you could harm their customers. Under the Fair Credit Reporting Act, as a potential employee, you're entitled to a copy of the report if the employer or potential employer uses the information from the credit or consumer report for an adverse action, such as denying you a job, terminating you as an employee, or denying you a promotion. You should ask for a copy of the credit report to make sure that there are no errors.

Many people find out that they are victims of identity theft when they're denied employment or a promotion, and they review a copy of their credit report. Unfortunately, most employers won't tell you that the reason they didn't hire you was because of your credit report, your consumer report, or your background check. Instead, they'll say that you don't have the qualifications that other candidates do, and that's why you weren't hired. That's why we suggest you get a background check yourself before you even apply for a job.

Authorizing Background Checks

- **Be prepared for a background check.**
  Remember, if an employer asks for your authorization to order a background check, and you refuse, then you'll look suspicious. Because of the epidemic of identity theft, your employer needs to know who he is hiring, and must take precautions to make sure that he is cautious with those he hires. This will minimize the company's risk of liability. Your background check could consist of two parts: First is your credit report that is filed with the credit reporting agencies, and second, is your consumer report, which is compiled by information brokers

and may include court records about you, Department of Motor Vehicle records, worker's compensation records, military records, incarceration records, educational records, state licensing records, drug test records, sex offender lists, and it could also include your character references. So, although you could check each of these individually by yourself, experts suggest you run a background check by a reputable company, because your employer is going to use either an in-house investigator or an outside information broker. Under the Fair Credit Reporting Act, your criminal convictions are reportable indefinitely. Think carefully before filing a workplace lawsuit like a worker's compensation case, disability case, workplace harassment case, etc., since these will be reported under civil cases, and many employers will be worried about hiring you. If a potential employer obtains your credit report or consumer report, (it must be with your permission), those reports are subject to the Fair Credit Reporting Act.

Here's another scenario of identity theft in the workplace that could come back to haunt you when you apply for a new job:

Steven had been working for XYZ Company for two years when he applied for a promotion. Upon investigating his background for this high-level promotion, the company found that Steven's name and Social Security number were associated with a man receiving unemployment compensation benefits. Steven was then contacted by a child support agency in a different county for failure to pay child support for an alleged child that he supposedly fathered in another state. Before the company would reconsider his promotion, he spent months trying to prove that he was a victim of identity theft.

Get Your Free Copy of Your Consumer Reports

Under recent federal law you are entitled to a free credit report from each of the credit reporting agencies. You can find the regulations with regard to this at the Federal Trade Commissions' web site: **www.ftc.gov** Also, under the Fair Credit Reporting Act, you are entitled to another free annual file disclosure for consumer reports that are prepared by a nation-wide specialty consumer reporting agency. This refers to the bigger companies that profile you with regard to your background check. These reports include your employment history, insurance, claims, etc. For those reports, prospective employees can obtain their consumer report maintained by the national specialty consumer reporting agencies. The big companies that provide employment background checks must set up a toll-free number to give you instructions on how to get the information on your file. Contact the Federal Trade Commission to find out which agencies will provide the free reports (**www.ftc.gov.**), and the toll-free number, which has not been established at the time of this printing.

- **Beware of fraudsters who may work under your name.** If someone is working using your name, they may be using your résumé, your business cards, your Social Security number, and information about your educational background to obtain jobs in your name. This could ruin your reputation, because they're not qualified to do the job that they are hired to do. We've heard from doctors, lawyers, accountants, nurses, and other professionals who learned that their identity had been stolen by someone for gainful employment. If you're about to change jobs, be conscious of this possibility. If there is a problem in getting a new position, order your Earnings and Benefits Statement form the Social Security Administration at

800 772-1213 or **www.ssa.gov**, and review the current earnings statement.

- **Notify potential references before you give their names to a potential employer.**
  Let references know what kind of job you're applying for. This way, if they're called and interviewed, they're not suspicious about why they are being called. You'll have a good idea of how comfortable they are regarding your background and skills and if you, indeed, want to use them. Additionally, you may be able to update them as to what you have been doing, and help them to clarify your talents. They may be able to protect you if, indeed, they're asked questions that refer to a background that clearly is not you, such as a criminal background.

Employee Protection— Privacy While Working

- **Be aware that your calls may be monitored.**
  Be aware that your calls may be monitored when speaking with clients, customers, or friends. A company may do this for "quality control." Normally a company will let you know that you are being monitored, however, because you're using their equipment, you must recognize that your conversations are not private. Be mindful that anything you say on a company telephone does not have the same protections as it does on your own telephone at home or even on your digital cell phone. Don't speak about confidential issues, or provide financial information on company property.

- **Be cautious of computer monitoring.**
  Your employer owns the computers that you use for work. Some employers and unscrupulous employees monitor your computer in such a way that they can see what is on your screen or they

monitor your keystrokes. They have access to the computer terminals and your hard disks. Legally, an employer can monitor your Internet usage and the e-mails that you send.

- **Don't use e-mails for non-business-related issues unless your employer authorizes you to do so.**
  Even if you are authorized to send some personal messages by e-mail, never include sensitive or confidential information that you would feel uncomfortable having anyone else see. Remember that your e-mail is like a postcard; the company or another employee could use that information to hurt you.

- **When using your voice mail system at work, don't assume that your conversations are private.**
  When leaving voice mails for other staff members, or if others leave messages for you, warn friends and family that your voice mail is not private.

- **Be cautious even when using encryption software.**
  When using encryption software on company equipment, remember that since it is a company device, even the encrypted e-mails that you send or the encrypted documents that you store on your computer are subject to monitoring by your employer. Your technology department or other employees may have access to your sensitive information. A fellow employee or even your boss could use your sensitive information for financial gain to hurt you.

Jane went to work for a small business. As required, she provided her Social Security number and all of her other identifying information. Unfortunately, the business wasn't doing well, and the owner had to let the business go. Soon afterwards, Jane found another position, but months later she learned that her identity had been stolen. Upon investigating where all of the credit lines, credit cards, and Internet purchases were sent, she learned that her former employer, whom she had trusted and who had access to all of her personal information, had stolen her identity.

- **Be wary of whom you share information with at work.** Since you spend most of your waking day in the workplace, it's easy for you to become trusting and oblivious to your vulnerability. Use extra caution with your personal documents, your paycheck stub (which usually has your Social Security number), your checkbooks, purses, Palm Pilots®, wallets, and briefcases; it's easy to let your guard down in a place where you know the staff. Don't be embarrassed to ask your employer and colleagues to take steps to minimize everyone's risk of identity theft.

  If your employer demands that you display your Social Security number or requires you to disclose unnecessary information —let them know that this may cause identity theft and expose them to legal consequences. If they don't believe you, show them this book! You may refer your company to Chapter Eight of this book, to educate your staff.

Protection Measures — Responsible Information Handling Practices

Below is an example of a doctor's client who called us with the disturbing story of his victimization:

Dr. George is a successful ophthalmologist. Without his knowledge, one of his part-time bookkeepers opened a bank account in another city using the doctor's name. He then deposited checks made out to the doctor into that account. The imposter then ordered $10,000 worth of eyeglasses, and thousands of dollars worth of equipment for the new office he had rented as Dr. George. For over a year, *while continuing to work for Dr. George, he diverted checks into the fraud account. He also ran a business under the name of Dr. George and prescribed eyeglasses. When the imposter didn't pay his bills, creditors and unhappy patients contacted the real Dr. George.*

The workplace is filled with myriad opportunities to commit identity theft. In fact, thieves get more information in and around the workplace than they do from stolen wallets or from the Internet. Most companies spend a great deal more on technology to protect company trade secrets than they do on limiting access to personal information or instituting proper information-handling practices. They often don't see how off-line information security adds to the bottom line. Security-related technology only addresses the technical problems. The non-technology issues must be a priority too. Privacy and security policies should be available to all employees to read the first day on the job. Every member of the organization needs to be aware of company procedures and values. Staff needs training and meetings about what they must do to protect the privacy, identity, and security of the entire corporation.

Audit your privacy work habits by asking the following questions. (If you don't work at a business—consider these questions when doing business with a company):

- Do all employees receive a copy of the company privacy policy? Is it described with specific examples so that everyone understands it and can implement it when speaking with fellow employees, customers, and clients?
- Do customers know and understand all policies?
- Are employees leaving sensitive documents on their desk when they leave for lunch or at the end of the day (or even for the bathroom)?
- What about their computer screens? Do employees know that

they must close a sensitive file and encrypt it when leaving their desks? Are they careful not to allow others to read their screen while working on a document?

- How does the company dispose of hard copies of sensitive information?
- How does the company dispose of computer hard drives, fax machines, back-up tapes, computer disks, and other media containing sensitive information?
- Are all employees aware of proper disposal, shredding, and overriding software?
- When employees are moving to a new office or leaving the business, is there someone available to make sure that sensitive information is erased? Is it discarded in a proper way?
- Does the company refrain from using the Social Security number of the client or customer when sending information through the mail? Is sensitive information exposed to others who don't need to see it?
- Is the Social Security number collected only when you absolutely must have it? For example, for tax reporting purposes?
- Does the company collect biometric information such as a fingerprint, iris scan, retina scans, hand or facial scans, or DNA? Where is it stored? How is it protected?
- When providing information for credit reporting agencies, what extra steps are taken to verify new customers before issuing them merchandise or credit?
- If the company learns of a security breach in which an employee or an outside person has accessed sensitive information about employees, customers, or clients, does the company immedi-

ately inform the potential victims of identity theft that their information has been accessed? Does the company provide them with information regarding fraud alerts on their credit report and how to protect themselves?

- Are access privileges removed, i.e. passwords changed, when employees or contractors leave their job or position?
- Is employee compliance with security and privacy policies and procedures considered during performance evaluations?
- What enforcement procedures and consequences are there for employees who violate security and privacy policies and procedures?
- Do you collect the absolute minimum amount of personal information necessary to accomplish what you need with your employees and customers? Do you only use the information for the purpose stated?
- Do you keep an inventory of all of your laptops, PDAs, computers, record systems, backup systems, and other storage media to verify if any sensitive information is missing? And can you trace back with a log and trail who has had control of all of those pieces of equipment?
- Do you train all new temporary independent contractors and vendors, including those you outsource to, in your privacy and security procedures, and do you monitor them?
- Do you outsource sensitive data to other nations? If so, what precautions do you take to protect that data? Do you let customers know who has their personal information?
- Do you have a written set of steps that are to be followed for the notification of all employees, customers, and others whose

unencrypted personal information has been acquired by an unauthorized person?

- Do you contact and cooperate fully with law enforcement to let them know about any possible security breaches or identity theft cases?
- When customers, clients, and employees are concerned about their privacy or the availability of their information to others, do you provide a privacy officer or customer service representative, for information, assistance, and guidance?
- For more information about recommended practices, notification of security breaches, and how businesses can protect their customers and consumers, visit the Office of Privacy Protection for California's Department of Consumer Affairs at **www.privacy.ca.gov** and click on Recommended Practices in the Notification of Security Breaches and the Recommended Practices for the Protection of the Social Security Number, and Recommended Practices For Data Sharing.

Secure the Physical Environment For Your Business

Identity thieves and other criminals often do their business through physical intrusion. Since it's so easy to capture sensitive information, your first line of defense must be the physical environment at work!

Ensure the physical security of your sensitive information.

Answer these questions:

- Do you use privacy screens around computer terminals?

- Do you lock doors to cabinets and offices with sensitive information?
- Do you utilize alarms and security curtains?
- Do you ask visitors to identify themselves, wear badges, and log in and out?
- How do you restrict access to rooms with personnel files, and cabinets with sensitive information and trade secrets?
- Do you implement a log and password or biometric entry key to enter the sensitive areas and lock doors and windows (close curtains) when they're not in use?
- Do you keep track of the serial numbers of computers, laptops, PDAs, fax machines, copiers, etc., so that they can be identified and recovered if they're stolen?
- Do you set up secure printers and secure faxes for confidential information?
- How do you enforce a clean desk policy to make sure that whenever employees leave their desks any sensitive or personal information that they have been working on is stored away in a locked file?
- Do you maintain a list of rules for staff regarding what equipment your employees can take offsite, and do you have a sign-in / sign-out process for all such items?

Outsourcing to other companies and other nations

How do you make sure that any company you outsource to or contract with will abide by all of your privacy and security procedures to protect the sensitive information of your customers and clients?

Concerns about outsourcing to foreign countries: Identity theft in our own country is out of control. Law enforcement in the U. S. doesn't have the resources to deal with all of the millions of victims. For the best protection of your staff and your customers, consider not outsourcing sensitive information to a foreign country. We have no control over police agencies of any other country, and our own law enforcement is overwhelmed with our own identity thieves. Only about 10 percent of identity theft cases are investigated in our country. It's already a challenging process for identity theft victims to clear their credit and regain their life in our own society. The issues regarding re-establishing your identity are multiplied a thousand fold if you are victimized by a foreign fraudster. Just imagine dealing with foreign cultures and languages that you don't understand to try and prove your innocence of financial theft or some other crime. Worse yet, consider the chances that terrorists could have access to your sensitive information while it is stored in economically disadvantaged countries such as India, Pakistan, and Jamaica where much of the outsourcing is taking place.

Although it may be profitable to use much less expensive labor outside of our country (to process sensitive data and financial data on American citizens), it exposes your customers to a much higher risk of loss and greater vulnerability if their personal information is accessed. When outsourcing, your company has far less control over the policies and procedures in a far away land. Although some companies say they are opening branches in foreign countries, foreign law enforcement is not controlled or enforced by our laws or your companies. Even if you have contractual agreements as to specific requirements and protection for personal and sensitive information, who will ensure enforcement?

Further Protection For Business Owners and Their Employees

Angry employees may insidiously cause identity theft for revenge. Here is a vicious example of identity theft caused by an insider:

> *Paul, who worked in the human resources department, stayed late one evening. He made copies of the personal information in Richard's file (one of the high-paid executives). Paul wasn't fond of Richard, so he sold that information to someone who stole the executive's identity and caused him years of anguish in cleaning up the financial mess.*

Obviously, we cannot give you a failsafe way to protect yourself and your workplace associates because we can't control mal-intentioned human behavior. Besides, savvy imposters create new technologies and tricks every day. However, the following steps can help you create a much safer environment, give you greater peace of mind, and provide more control over confidential information.

- **Conduct criminal and civil background checks, including credit reports, before hiring employees who will have access to personal information—even if they're part-time or independent contractors.**
  Also, carefully screen cleaning services and temporary firms that your company utilizes. Several years ago, CBS television hired a cleaning crew that turned out to be a Nigerian fraud ring. The after-hours cleaning people "cleaned up" the trash, dumpster dived and rifled the desks of many of the top correspondents, and robbed them of their identity.

  We all want to believe that most people are honest and trustworthy. Unfortunately, we need to temper our trust with caution and inquiry. Your company could be held legally liable for negligent hiring if a victim of identity theft can trace the crime back to one of your employees who has a criminal background that you failed to detect. (For legal guidelines on conducting background checks, visit the Federal Trade Commission web site at **www.ftc.gov** and read the fact sheets at **www.privacyrights.org**.)

- **Keep all personal information about employees in locked cabinets and encrypted data files. Establish data security procedures for those who have access to the files.**
  Only specific persons with up-to-date training and need-to-know status should have access to personal files. When an employee does access information, there should be an audit trail so it is clear who accessed particular information and when. Confidential files should be segregated and locked in cabinets. There should be procedures to prevent ex-employees from gaining access to paper and computer files. Passwords must be changed when employees leave.

- **Limit the use of personal identifiers.**
  The use of the Social Security number for identification and record-keeping exposes those individuals to the risk of identity theft. Use an alternative number for employees and customers. Don't display personal data on documents that are widely seen by others, such as mailing labels. Access codes or personal identification numbers (PINs) should not be birth dates or Social Security numbers. Badges should never include the Social Security number.

- **Put photos on business cards for identification. (It's also good marketing.)**

One imposter stole an attorney's business cards from the receptionist's desk. The imposter used the business cards along with other false identification to steal thousands of dollars in credit and parade as a lawyer, potentially ruining the reputation of the victim. That attorney recommends using photo business cards.

It's very easy for the fraudster to obtain business cards and pretend to be you or one of your employees; with a current-looking photo, business cards are easy and inexpensive to make.

- **Adopt secure methods of disposing of personal information.**
  Industrial shredders should be used at large offices. Provide a personal crosscut shredder at each workstation or at least locked garbage bins. Place shredders near photocopiers, shared printers, and fax machines. For companies that outsource the shredding of documents, be careful to keep the material locked up until pickup in a secure area. Find out if the shredding company uses strict security procedures. (Recycling is not "shredding.")

  "Shredding" software should be used to delete confidential information from computer files. When disposing of computers, diskettes, magnetic tapes, and hard drives, erase them with a proven "wipe" function, or physically destroy them. In some states like California, Wisconsin and Georgia there are very strict document destruction laws. Federal law is also addressing the need for complete destruction of financial documents before discarding. Any company that does not completely destroy confidential or personal information before discarding it exposes itself to lawsuits if anyone is injured as a result.

Thousands of California State University students and graduate students and staff were stunned to learn that their personal information may have been stolen when a computer hard drive belonging to the CSU auditor turned up missing. The hard drive was either discarded or stolen, and it contained personal information, including 23,000 names and Social Security numbers. According to the auditor, the hard drive was placed in a secure room for the night, and when staff members returned the next day and it was gone. Better information-protection systems probably would have prevented this.

- **Train designated staff about security procedures in sending sensitive personal information by fax.**
  Only authorized persons should be allowed to send sensitive documents by fax. All faxes should have a confidential cover sheet (prohibiting re-disclosure), and the fax number should be double-checked before sending. Always call the recipient before sending to let them know that confidential information is arriving, ask them to go to the fax machine to receive it, and acknowledge receipt afterwards. Place shredders near fax machines.

- **No one should leave or send personal, confidential, or sensitive information by voice mail, cellular phones, pagers, answering machines, or e-mail.**
  None of these transmissions is private or secure unless encrypted or sent via a secure network. Remember, any stored messages could someday be used as evidence in a lawsuit. According to the courts, unless company policy says that you do have privacy for your e-mails or voice mail, you do not have privacy. When using company machines and equipment, your voice mails and e-mails belong to the organization and may be accessed at any time. Even your Internet surfing history and keystrokes may be monitored.

- **Use designated, secure printers and copiers for confidential information, with shredders located nearby.**
  Care must be taken to prevent sending confidential information

to the wrong printer. Draft copies should be shredded when no longer needed.

- **Adopt a written privacy protection policy that covers all persons within the organization and applies to dealings with persons outside the organization.**
  All employees, and even your board of trustees, should be trained in the company's security measures and privacy protection policies. Review these policies and update them regularly, followed by retraining. Even temporary and part-time employees, independent consultants, and vendors should be subject to the written policies and should acknowledge their understanding and commitment. For employees working at home or away from the office on trips, training should include special guidelines for information-handling offsite.

  It is beyond the scope of this book to provide comprehensive information security and privacy strategies for all of your needs. For specific information as to your own particular needs, consult the appropriate trade and professional associations, experts in your field, libraries, and bookstores. Consider hiring a privacy and security expert to help you specifically design a privacy plan to audit your company's unique situation.

Protecting Workplace Technology

In Chapter Two you read about the concerns for technology dangers for your home computer. Your business computer is far more vulnerable. Not only are you and your company exposed to danger, but also your legal exposure extends to employees, customers, and clients who may be potential victims. Additionally, trade secrets, patents, and other confidences are vulnerable to malicious hackers. Businesses also can become victims of identity theft—false web sites, e-mails, and files may be set up to steal the identity of a company. Businesses are at risk whether there is an off-line or online security breach.

Following are some steps you can use in the workplace to defend your virtual world. Large businesses have whole departments dedicated to technology, but small businesses and independent contractors normally don't have the resources to set up technology-secure departments.

The following tasks will minimize your risk of loss:

- **Carefully screen your computer consultant or outside security professional.**
  Carefully screen any security expert or computer consultant you hire to make sure that person is who he claims to be. After all, you're giving him access to all your sensitive files and to your whole network; you must be able to trust him. Obviously, large corporations must require that employees in their technology departments undergo background checks. Use audit trails to assure that a disgruntled employee or contractor doesn't betray the business or steal identities.

- **Make sure that every computer has antivirus software.**
  Update it weekly, and run it every night. Search for viruses and delete them or quarantine them. You should use only the current year's software, with the newest innovations to protect your computer and your data. The software should automatically download the latest definitions from the Internet.

- **Train your entire staff to never open any suspicious file attached to an e-mail from any unknown or untrustworthy source.**
  In fact, unless the attachment is specifically described in the e-mail, even if the e-mail comes from a known source, it should

not be opened but rather deleted. Instead, contact the person who sent it and ask them to describe what they were sending in the e-mail and ask them to resend it.

- **Require all members of your staff to use the security features provided with their e-mail programs.**
  Always check out the most current patches for all of the software that you use, whether it's financial software, Windows programs, or any other programs.

- **Set up an e-mail notification or have automatic notices of updates.**
  Run a weekly update of all your software. Calendar the updates to make sure that you are getting all of the proper patches, which will decrease your vulnerability to holes in your software that could allow in viruses (programs that reproduce themselves by infecting other programs, causing damage such as erasing files or even an entire hard drive).

- **Install hardware and software firewalls that block all the traffic between the Internet and your network.**
  If you want your network to be invisible to the outside, you'll install these hardware firewalls to hide the addresses of computers behind the firewall. The firewall connects between the cable or DSL modem in the computers on your network. Although a firewall is a great line of defense, note, it's not going to protect you against attacks from the inside and data that's coming in legitimately.

- **Use complex passwords.**
  Change them every 90 days, or sooner if an employee leaves. Include a combination of lower and upper case letters, numbers, and symbols.

- **Back up all of your files daily.**

Don't let a catastrophe happen if your computer crashes. What would you do if you suddenly lost all of your data? How would you do business? To recover as quickly as possible, you must have backups.

- **Get business insurance for your computer.**
  Computer insurance will reimburse you for money you spend to restore your data if there is a "crash."
- **Take extra precautions if you have a wireless network.**
  WiFi uses a radio link instead of cables to connect computers. So, anyone within range can pick up the data on the network. "Drive-by" hacking can occur when an intruder is driving by or is across the street from your business. If you're using your laptop on the Internet at Starbuck's, a hacker could easily pick up and "sniff" for insecure networks. Make sure that everyone on the wireless, whether it is on his or her laptop, PDA, or on the PC has configured the security features that are built into the wireless network. Many manufactures don't automatically have the security device turned on as the network is easier to use if it's turned off.
- **Restrict the network access to trusted addresses.**
  The network card for each computer has a unique code that is your immediate access control address. The network can set up connection points to restrict the network to particular control addresses so you can filter out unknown intruders.

Be Cautious When Allowing Your Employees to Work From Home or Remote Locations

It's a great convenience to work at home but, at the same time, if your employees can tap into your system, there is a concern that unauthorized hackers can also enter the system. When you allow your employees to connect remotely to check e-mail and access files, you're also significantly increasing your security risk. To be safe, consider setting up a VPN (Virtual Private Network). When you use this method, the data that is sent is encrypted when it travels over the Internet, and it restricts outsiders from being able to read it. To set this up, you're going to need a computer security professional.

- **Consider quality biometrics for access to systems.** Security experts believe that strong passwords aren't enough. They suggest biometric codes (like fingerprints or hand scans). There should be authentication to confirm the identity of all users who are going to connect to your network. Make sure that you set up safeguards for any biometric information you use and require a password as a secondary verification.

  Whether you work in a small business or a large corporation, computers and security issues will put your business at risk. Computer savvy crooks have many techniques to steal data. You'll need to educate yourself and your staff about how to protect yourselves, your colleagues, your customers, and your employees from malicious outside intruders as well as unscrupulous employees.

Protective Measures For Your Customers and Clients

Charles became the victim of an imposter who opened up several credit accounts in his name. He traced the identity thief back to one of the employees at his health club, a man with a forgery conviction in his background. The crook was aided in his misdeeds by the health club, because it uses the Social Security number as the member number. Charles sued the health club for negligent hiring, and failing to screen its employees who are given access to sensitive personal information.

If you are like most American consumers, you're becoming increasingly concerned about your lack of control over your personal information and decreased privacy. A recent Business Week Harris Poll found that 53 percent of the respondents believe that laws should be passed to specify how personal information can be collected and used.

Your customers and clients trust you and rely on you to protect their personal information. Your company may have legal exposure for failing to protect someone's privacy if damages result from your failure to act in a responsible manner.

The following steps will help your company establish responsible information-handling practices in order to avoid putting your customers and clients at risk for identity theft.

1. **Display your privacy protection policy in your literature and on your company's web site.**
   This will afford customers and clients an opportunity to communicate concerns and complaints regarding the use of their information. Assign an individual or a department the responsibility for your information-handling and privacy policies. Designate a "privacy officer" to handle these concerns. Assistance should be easily accessible to your customers, not shielded by a complicated voice mail system.

2. **Train your employees about identity theft sensitivity.**
   When an identity theft victim contacts your company (regarding fraud in connection with your organization) make sure your customer service and fraud departments are well trained and know how to advise this individual. By helping the victim clear his or her record, you will limit your legal exposure as to the

victim and provide a valuable service. If your company cooperates with law enforcement and there is a criminal conviction of the imposter, your company's financial losses may be recouped by a court order for monetary restitution.

3. **Don't share, sell, or transmit data about customers without their prior permission.**
   Guarding that information will also limit your legal exposure if that information subjects your customers to identity theft.

4. **Limit your company's data collection to the information necessary for the stated purpose and nothing more.**
   Avoid the practice of collecting sensitive customer information just because you "might need it someday." Only collect what you absolutely need, and let your customers know why you need it, and the purpose for collecting it.

5. **Provide customer / client inspection.**
   Your customers should have the right to inspect and correct (and delete if appropriate) their personal information in your possession. This practice will not only increase customers' trust in your information-handling practices, it will improve the accuracy of your files.

6. **Make sure that any person you are dealing with is truly the customer he or she claims to be.**
   Businesses lose hundreds of millions of dollars each year as a result of computer crime, credit fraud, and identity theft. For example, when a customer pays by credit and tells you he or she has moved, verify the change of address with a phone call to the previous phone number, and / or send a note to the former address to see if a move was really made. Carefully scrutinize suspicious documents. If you grant credit, never issue instant

credit without taking adequate steps to verify identity, including a photo ID with an address, which can be compared with the address on the applicant's credit report. It's a good idea to ask for three pieces of identification.

7. **Take every opportunity to become informed about privacy issues, fraud, and identity theft.**

   Join a local financial crimes group. Your police or sheriff's department can inform you of such groups. Invite law enforcement to speak to your employees at a luncheon. Provide in-house training by local experts in the field of identity theft.

   Obtain training materials developed by security-related professional associations and by credit card companies such as VISA, MasterCard, and American Express. Visit web sites containing business-oriented security information. The U.S. Secret Service, for example, offers fraud-prevention tips for businesses, **www.treas.gov/us**. Please also refer to other resources listed in Chapter Eight.

Be Positive, Persistent, Patient, and Service-oriented

As should be clear now, you must be vigilant in protecting yourself and others in commerce. Government agencies, banks, credit grantors, and small businesses are made up of people just like you. So, if you are worried that your policies may be seen as overly intrusive or inconvenient (verifying identification for example), explain your concerns about identity theft, and be enthusiastic about trying to protect the people you encounter. If customers are fearful about providing information to you, truthfully apprise them of your privacy policies, and explain how your company will safeguard their information. Don't encourage anyone to divulge unnecessary information that makes him or her feel uncomfortable. It's good business strategy to be sensitive to privacy and identity theft protection. Protecting privacy builds trust and trust builds quality, enduring business relationships.

Chapter Five

Better Mousetraps: Products That Can Protect You

"For a list of all the ways technology has failed to improve the quality of life, please press three."

— Alice Kahn

Most of us joke about being tethered to our pagers and cell phones, and about what a pain technology is, but in reality, we're lucky to have such a wide range of products and tools available to help us safeguard our identities and protect our privacy. The process of protection includes using these tools to help you implement a personal privacy plan. You may already own many of the items listed below and may not even realize that their use will help give you greater peace of mind. Audit yourself as to what products you already have and what you may wish to consider adding to your Privacy Protection Plan. The items listed here, some of which were mentioned earlier, apply to the workplace as well as the home.

Please contact us at **www.identitytheft.org** with any additional ideas for creative products to use that will ensure greater protection of your personal information. We welcome your input.

1. Discarding, receiving, and storing personal information

- **Personal paper document shredder**
  Destroy financial information, pre-approved credit offers, account statements and other confidential data. Portable compact shredders are available for businesspersons on the road.

- **Locking mailbox or a box at a post office**
  Safeguard your billing statements, checks, and other confidential mail from the growing problem of mail theft.

- **Home safes**
  Secure your passport, Social Security card, estate plan, and other personal information, since these items are "jewels" to an identity thief.

- **Lockboxes and locking file cabinets, drawers, and closets**
  Protect your home office, which contains myriad pieces of confidential information. A visitor, repairperson, cleaning service, babysitter, home healthcare attendant, or worse, a burglar, may access your personal data if it is left unguarded. Take an extra moment to put this information under lock and key.

- **Portable locking security chests—fireproof**
  Keep your valuables, including your computer backup, safe from thieves and fire.

- **Security envelopes and tamper-proof mailers**
  Never mail any classified or confidential information from your home or office without using security envelopes with a tint or lining that ensures confidentiality. For larger documents, use tear-proof mailers that inhibit tampering.

- **Security systems—for home and vehicles (alarm systems, security lighting)**
  Identity thieves want to invade your home for your valuable information. Even if you don't install a comprehensive alarm system, install security lighting that acts as a motion alarm. Put locks on all windows so that if you slightly open windows for cool air, the window locks prevent entry. Adopt a dog to warn of intruders and to guard your residence.

2. Protection products to use in public places

- **Fanny pack and/or undergarment security pouch**
  When traveling, guard your passport and other identifying information by keeping them on your person.

- **Valet key for your car that does not open the trunk or glove compartment**
  Limit access to personal information when you park with a valet, and never leave papers, briefcase, or suitcases on the seats.

- **Automobile alarm**
  Always lock your car, and consider arming it with a burglar alarm to protect your valuable personal information inside.

- **Locking briefcase with alarm and tracking device**
  Secure your sensitive personal and business information while on the road.

3. Services to consider for protecting personal information

- **"Pay by Phone" service for your bills**
  Find out about this service from your bank. It eliminates your worry about mail theft, usually costs less than the cost of stamps, and saves you time and effort as well.

- **Voice mail system**
  For more privacy of your telephone messages when you are unavailable, consider using voice mail with a private password or security code. Be aware that your voice mail system at work is not private and may be accessed by your employer and others.

- **Telephone Caller ID and Anonymous Call Rejection**
  Consider subscribing to the phone company's Caller ID and Anonymous Call Rejection features to find out who is really on the line. Don't provide personal information to someone you do not know. Keep in mind that Caller ID is a double-edged sword regarding privacy. Many consumers do not wish to divulge their phone number, which may be unlisted.

- **Credit card security cancellation service**
  If your wallet is lost or stolen, you can make just one call to immediately alert credit grantors to the possibility of fraud.

- **Credit activity reporting service—Credit monitoring**
  As suggested in Chapter Two, you should order your credit report at least twice a year and look for fraud or mistakes. Once a year, under federal law, you may order your credit profile for free from each of the three major credit reporting agencies (**www.experian.com**; **www.equifax.com**; **www.transunion.com**). Alternatively, for about $60-$120 a year, you can subscribe to a credit monitoring service that offers quarterly access to your credit report and/or notifies you when there has been a credit inquiry or if negative information has been added to your profile. Some services permit monitoring online at their web sites or by e-mail. If you use such a service, make sure it combines information from all three major credit reporting agencies: Equifax, Experian, and Trans Union.

4. Protection products for home and office computers

➢ **Diskettes and CD ROM, DVDs, and external hardware**
Use these for sensitive files that you do not want to store on your hard drive. If you don't keep financial and confidential files on your hard drive, you have less to worry about when connected to a network or the Internet.

➢ **Locking disk boxes**
Guard your backup disks and sensitive information on disk by keeping the material stored in secured boxes or locked file cabinets separate from other information.

➢ **Locking cables to prevent equipment theft**
If your computer is stolen, all your personal information will be in the hands of a criminal. Use locking cables to secure all your computer equipment. Be aware that some thieves only steal the memory cards from inside the computer, leaving the computer in place. In such cases, cables are not effective. But file protection products, discussed below, can prevent thieves from reading your stolen files

➢ **Security backup systems**
Install a backup system to copy your hard drive in case of loss or theft. Keep a backup "offsite" in case of fire or theft. You'll know what information has been stolen and be able to take proactive measures to prevent fraud. Don't forget to back-up your laptop too.

➢ **Use anonymous software**
Surf anonymously—download software that allows you to visit web sites without revealing your identity if you participate in Usenet news groups. If you share your computer with family, friends, or coworkers, obtain a software program that protects sensitive files with password access. If you participate

in Usenet news groups, obtain software that allows you to be anonymous (i.e. **www.anonymizer.com**).

- **Run antivirus software to keep your computer virus-free.** To protect your computer from malicious codes, which can destroy files, the software must be updated continuously and run each day. It must scan your drives, removable media, data files, and most important... your e-mail.
- **Purchase and update all your software, and download patch programs.**
  Old software can cause you problems. Hackers creatively look for vulnerability; regularly download patches from the manufacturer so you are shielded.
- **Use anti-key logging software that can detect key logging programs (www.anti-keylogger.com)**
  Key loggers report and monitor your keystrokes without you knowing it; this is a form of spyware. Download anti-spy software and other software to detect and remove adware and spyware. These programs alert you about, and let you eliminate, software that comes into your computer without your knowledge. Spyware records and sends information from your computer to remote sites.

5. **Other products for protection of personal information in the workplace**

- **Industrial shredders with maximum-security capability**
  Use these at large offices with a need for maximum security. As I already suggested, place shredders at copier machines, fax machines, and in individual offices. Sensitive personal and business information should never be discarded without destruction. For maximum protection, use crosscut shredders that reduce paper to small dots.

- **Shredding services**
  Set up a schedule to have confidential files and boxes, old computer disks, etc. destroyed. (It's best to get a service that brings a truck to shred on-site.)
- **Locking waste baskets**
  For offices with centralized shredding machines or a scheduled shredding service, it is crucial to safeguard sensitive information until it is destroyed.
- **Security locking for phone systems**
  Keep telephone equipment in a locked room with a security locking system. Inspect it regularly for tampering or eavesdropping.
- **Security screens for monitors**
  In busy offices, especially those with access by the public, security screens ensure that others cannot see what you are working on unless they are right in front of the screen.
- **Privacy Protection Panels**
  Use privacy panels when several employees are working in close proximity to make the work area more private when walls are not possible.
- **Screensavers with password protection**
  These enable you to leave your computer unattended. Once the screensaver is activated, your computer cannot be accessed without the proper password.
- **Photo identification badges**
  Protect your employees from others taking their identity and having access to data that is restricted.
- **Photo business cards**
  Use photo business cards to protect your identity and make a lasting impression.

➢ **Biometrics for authentication of identity.**
This technology presents both privacy vulnerability as well as safeguards. It is meant to verify that the person using the computer (or the person wanting access, information, credit, or other services) is really the person he or she claims to be.

Biometrics uses measurable physiological characteristics, such as fingerprints, scans of facial features, iris or retina scans, or DNA. For example, your fingerprint can be recorded by a program in a computer and stored in a database. To identify you at a later time, the computer will scan your fingerprint and search for a match in the database. If the system can verify your identity, you will be granted access. Unfortunately, there are many false positives and false negatives.

With identity theft on the rise, proponents of biometrics view this type of identification as a fail-safe authentication method. Since biometrics technology is still being developed, its accuracy is not assured, and safeguards have not been completely tested, so we're cautiously watchful of it. Our privacy could be jeopardized unless strict guidelines are enacted so that the information is not bought, shared, sold, or corrupted—to our detriment. In other words, the same problems we presently have with abuses in using our Social Security numbers could happen with our fingerprints, facial scans, etc.

Use of this technology is a growing trend in banks, government agencies, and large corporations. The newer U.S. passports are embedded with a computer chip that holds a traveler's digitized photo and fingerprints. They are to be scanned by customs agents at an airport or border crossing, popping up a photo on a screen. "Trusted traveler" airline programs require biometric information to verify who you are. We're concerned that it's not foolproof (accuracy is not

100 percent); Biometrics is invasive, and it may be subject to corruption by hackers, especially when information is transmitted electronically or stored without strict security. According to technology columnist Simon L. Garfinkel, "We'll be seeing more of this technology and it will be seeing more of us in the near future. Best to keep an eye out."

6. **Other protection ideas for the workplace**

- **Provide training in identity theft and privacy protection**
  Hire security and privacy experts to provide training for your employees. Make sure that these professionals teach your staff how to guard your business identity and trade secrets, and how to protect the identity and privacy of your employees, clients, suppliers, and customers.

- **Develop your own privacy protection handbooks**
  These can be tailored to meet the specific needs of your business. Get help from the Federal Trade Commission at **www.ftc.gov**. You can also find help at **www.privacyassociation.org**. (The Independent Association of Privacy Professionals. Phone: (800) 266-6501) Considering hiring a privacy and security professional to coach you in developing your handbook.

- **Create a list of supplies for your company's privacy protection campaign**
  We have shared a list of general items to consider in instituting your privacy and identity theft awareness campaign. Wherever you have someone's personal information or sensitive business data, consider how it may be accessed and used in an unauthorized manner. Take preventive measures to secure the data so it may not be used, transferred, or

destroyed without your consent. We encourage you and your staff to hold a brainstorming session to discuss better ways of keeping personal information and business secrets safe from those who may do harm.

What if your personal information is stolen and used fraudulently?

In Chapters Two, Three, Four, and Five, we focused on protection measures; but we've warned you that there is no guarantee that your information won't be accessed, even if you have taken every precaution. In Chapter Six we'll prepare you for the possibility of dealing with the crisis of identity theft and show you how you can overcome that challenge.

Chapter Six

Take It Back: How To Regain Your Identity and Financial Health

"We should be careful to get out of an experience only the wisdom that is in it—and stop there; lest we be like the cat that sits down on a hot stove-lid. She will never sit down on a hot stove-lid again—and that is well; but also she will never sit down on a cold one anymore. "

— Mark Twain

The worst has happened; despite all your best efforts, you have become a victim of identity theft. What do you do now? Unfortunately, victims themselves are burdened with resolving the problem. It is important to act quickly and assertively to minimize the damage. This chapter walks you through the steps you must take to regain your identity and financial health.

But remember, each identity theft case is different; you may not have to take every step listed in this chapter, only those that apply to your situation.

The one small comfort in enduring your situation is that you are generally protected by federal law from paying the imposter's bills. You are liable for only the first $50 of your losses, and most financial institutions will waive even that amount.

You do need to deal immediately with the details of your case, because, for one thing, the identity thief may be continuing his or her crime spree even as you read this. Further, by delaying action, you could complicate the case. A stolen credit card, for example, may change hands, making the trail harder to follow. The perpetrator may travel to a distant state or country, adding to the jurisdictional hurdles even as he or she orders new cards and gets more instant credit. Further, some legal remedies can expire if you don't act within a certain time period.

Please remember that you should not pay an imposter's bills in your name, (even if it is a family member who robbed you); you could be left with a bad credit report and months, if not years, of trying to restore your financial health. You also may be hassled by bill collectors, banks, merchants, and others. You'll need to convince them that an imposter —not you—made the purchases, filed the bankruptcy, rented the apartment, or committed the crime.

Don't expect help from authorities in your quest to set matters straight; it's a self-help challenge, which means well-organized files are vital. If you feel overwhelmed by all this legal "mumbo jumbo" and letter writing, you may wish to obtain our book, From *Victim to Victor: A Step-by-Step Guide to Ending the Nightmare of Identity Theft,* Second Edition with CD (Porpoise Press, Inc., 2004), which includes a CD with logs, forms, and all the attorney-composed letters you need to complete—just fill in the blanks and send the letters (return receipt requested). You'll also have the steps to take and resources. If you can't do the work yourself, our guide will save you hundreds of hours and thousands of dollars in attorney fees.

Following are some actions you need to take:

Taking On The Challenge

No one can really take on this challenge for you entirely, not even a lawyer! You're the only one who knows your credit and financial picture, such as which are the fraudulent accounts and which are the actual accounts. So it's up to you to act quickly and assertively to minimize the damage. In all dealings with the authorities and with financial institutions, remember to:

- Keep a clipboard with a log of every conversation, including dates, names, and phone numbers. Otherwise, you're sure to get confused as to who said what and when. (There are logs on the CD that comes with the book *From Victim to Victor*). Make several copies and keep them up-to-date.
- Log all time and expenses, too. Make a note of time spent and expenses incurred. You'll need such information if you eventually seek reimbursement for damages in settlement or legal actions against companies who may have acted inappropriately. You'll also need this for information for a judge if your impostor is caught and ordered to reimburse you. Also, your fraud losses and out-of-pocket costs may be tax deductible under the IRS Code 165e.
- When you call any agency, get the name of the supervisor of the fraud department. Ask also for his / her direct phone line, fax numbers, and e-mail address. Don't waste time telling your story to someone with no authority to take action. Even if the supervisor isn't available to speak to you, ask for a return phone call—this saves tremendous time and aggravation in follow-up.
- Confirm all phone conversations in writing. (Employees you

speak to may leave, be transferred, or be negligent in follow-up.)

- Always send correspondence by certified mail (return receipt requested). This is important to show notification and to document that correspondence was received. Note in your log the date items were received, since it may be a legal issue later (i.e. timelines and statute of limitations issues.)
- Keep copies of all letters and documents in organized files in banker boxes in a safe place.
- Complete the Uniform Affidavit developed by the Federal Trade Commission, it is also in the Resource Section at the end of this book, and update it regularly as you learn new information about your case.

Twenty Steps You Must Take Now!

To help ease your burden as you deal with restoring your finances and good name, we've created 20 steps you should take as soon as possible. (Not all 20 steps apply to every victim, so you'll need to pick and choose. If, for example, your case doesn't involve a civil judgment against you, you might skip step one about dealing with the civil court.) Plus, these can serve as guidelines should new problems arise at a later date.

This list may look daunting; in reality, it will save you time and empower you for what's to come later. For your own sake, you must do a thorough job. The identity you save will be your own! Remember, each step must be followed up in writing—to keep a paper trail and protect you. The resources to contact for each step are listed in Chapter Eight.

Step 1: Contact the credit bureaus.

Immediately call the fraud units of the three major credit reporting firms: TransUnion, Equifax, and Experian. You need to contact all three because each may have a different version of your credit report. Recent federal law states that to place a fraud alert, you need to call only one bureau and that agency will contact the other two, but it is safer to call all three to make sure you have protected your rights.

You'll get an automated voice recording prompt which will allow you to add a fraud alert and receive a free credit report. You will be asked to punch in your Social Security number. Be sure to listen to all choices, as the menu can be very confusing. If your situation involves an imposter who's opening up new accounts in your name, write the credit bureau and alert them that your identity has been used to obtain credit that you haven't applied for. Request that a fraud alert be placed in your report immediately and remain in effect for seven (7) years. The bureaus will automatically place a fraud alert good for at least 90 days, according to federal law. (See our resources list in Chapter Eight for contact information for the three major credit-reporting agencies).

Remember, if you're a victim of identity fraud, or if you have been denied credit, insurance, or employment because of something on your credit report, you're entitled to a free credit report. It's the law. (You're also entitled to a free credit report if you're unemployed or receiving welfare.) Recent federal law will allow everyone in the United States to get a free credit report once a year from each of the three credit reporting agencies. The agencies must establish a toll-free number for non-victims, which you will find on their web sites.

Points to make in your follow-up letter to the credit bureaus:

- Ask that your account be flagged as one on which fraud is suspected. Make sure to ask how long the fraud alert will be posted on your account, and how you can extend it if necessary. Ask that it be kept on there for at least seven years, as federal law allows.

- Depending on your state law, you may be entitled to a security freeze. Some states like California, Texas, Louisiana, and others are passing laws that would entitle you to take your profile offline so a fraudster cannot get credit—and neither can you, without providing a PIN to allow your credit report to be reviewed by a creditor. Placing a security freeze on your credit reports essentially prevents anyone from accessing your credit file for any reason, until and unless you instruct the credit bureaus to unfreeze or "thaw" your report with a password. A freeze provides more protection than a fraud alert. If your identity thief won't cease to use your identity to obtain credit and companies are ignoring the fraud alert, and if you live in a state that allows this, you should consider using the security freeze to curtail access to your credit file. The security freeze is free to victims of identity theft. Non-victims who wish to use the security freeze for prevention purposes must pay a fee to activate the freeze in California. Not all states permitting freezes will allow non-victims to freeze their reports. Check out your state's laws at **www.consumer.gov/idtheft**.

- Add a "victim's statement" to your report, up to 100 words. Something like: "Someone has used my identification to apply for credit fraudulently. Contact me at 123-456-7890, to verify all applications for credit in my name before extending credit. (We suggest you provide your cell phone, in case you want instant credit.) Please contact fraud investigator ________ at ________ Police Department, phone number ________." This will increase your credibility as to the fraud with creditors, and reputable companies will call you before issuing credit.

- Ask the credit bureaus, in writing, to provide you with free copies of your credit report (Federal law allows two free reports for a victim in one year). The credit bureaus must also provide you a free report with the corrections.
- Ask for immediate access to the names, addresses, and phone numbers of credit card companies and other credit grantors with whom fraudulent accounts have been opened.
- Request the credit bureaus remove all inquiries (lists of companies that received a copy of your credit report for the purpose of issuing you credit) that have been generated due to the fraudulent access. Get the names, addresses, and phone numbers of all companies who made any inquiries listed on your credit report. These fraudulent inquiries must be removed because they can negatively affect your credit rating. Creditors who received your credit report must be notified of the fraud so they don't issue credit to the impersonator!
- Ask the credit bureaus to notify those who have received your credit report in the last year (two years for employers), and alert them to the fraud information. Remember, a creditor may offer credit up to a year after receiving your information. So, you must be proactive and stop the fraud before it is extended.
- Send a letter immediately to the credit agencies summarizing your requests. Be aware, though, that these measures may not entirely stop an imposter from opening new fraudulent accounts. That's because some credit grantors offering instant credit do

not carefully screen your report for fraud alerts, although new federal law requires that creditors honor your alert.

- When your credit report arrives, carefully read the instructions that accompany it. There's a wealth of information on the report, and a close study will give you clues to the nature and extent of the fraud as well as possible cures. Scrutinize each report line by line. These reports require diligent study.

Deciphering your report.

- Verify that your Social Security number is correct and that your name is not misspelled. Check to see if there is a similar name on your profile. Inform the agencies of the fraud / error, or it will be reported to credit grantors incorrectly.
- Check your address to make sure it has not been changed to a fraudulent one. Check to see if former addresses are correct. Insist that any incorrect address(es) be removed from your credit report promptly and completely. Otherwise, pre-approved cards may be sent to the impersonator.
- Find the date of the opening of the first fraudulent account.
- Then look for inquiries, which appear prior to that first, unfamiliar account, i.e., which bank, credit card company, or mortgage firm received your report before the opening of the fraudulent account. Ask each such company (where fraud occurred) for a copy of the original application with the forged signature used to obtain credit in your name. Ask for all information and documentation they have for the fraud account. This may lead you to the impersonator. Under federal law, the companies must send you the information free of charge.

- Demand that credit bureaus notify all those companies who received your credit report in the last year. This will alert those merchants to the fraud, and, it's hoped, prevent them from issuing credit. The credit bureaus must also notify those who've made inquiries, so new accounts are not issued. Request copies of each of those notifications for your records.

- Request a list of phone numbers and addresses of every prospective creditor who received your history from the credit reporting agencies. You should notify these institutions of the fraud and ask them not to issue credit to the impersonator. Federal law now requires this.

- Ask that your name be taken off all "pre-approved" and promotional lists sold by the three credit reporting agencies for at least five (5) years (Federal law allows this.) Normally, your name and financial profile is sold by the credit reporting bureaus without your prior permission. (California and North Dakota now require permission first.) (You may also be on similar lists sold by creditors and banks. You should write to all your creditors to stop the promotions.) It's important to stop getting these "pre-approved" offers at your address or in your name at the fraud perpetrator's address because he/she can continue to fill out the applications and receive yet more credit in your name. You can also call 1-888-5OPTOUT.

Step 2: Alert all creditors

Immediately call your creditors—especially those with whom you believe your name has been used fraudulently, and follow up in writing.

Make sure to request:

- Cancellation of the fraud accounts and removal of all fraudulent information on your credit reports. These negative accounts allow for more fraud and lower your credit score.

- Replacement cards with new account numbers for only your accounts that were used fraudulently. Ask that each of your true closed accounts be labeled as "account closed at consumer's request." (That's better than saying, "card lost or stolen" because that phraseology when reported to credit bureaus might imply that you're to blame for the loss, and may affect your credit score.)
- All documentation of the account, including:
  - Initial application with forged signature.
  - All billing statements.
  - Address and phone number where the cards were sent.
  - All correspondence between the fraudster and the creditor.
  - Any other information relative to the case.

  Federal law allows the victim, (upon presenting proper identification, a law enforcement report, and a completed Federal Trade Commission Affidavit), to obtain the above information free of charge within 30 days of the written request. The victim may also designate a law enforcement agency to receive this as well.
- Copies of transmittals from creditor to credit reporting agencies and collection agencies documenting removal of the fraud from your credit report profile.
- Placement of fraud alerts on all of your true bank accounts, investment accounts, retirement accounts, and credit cards or lines of credit. Put a new password on all such accounts. Do not use your mother's maiden name anymore, since it is on your

birth certificate, which is public record, and can be accessed on the Internet. (Use a new password in place of your mother's maiden name for each account.)

Remember: Don't cancel any real accounts of yours unless fraud has been committed on that account. This will only look more suspicious in the future and may make it more difficult for you to get credit later. Don't cancel your good cards!

If you must cancel a card due to fraud, loss, or theft, order a new card (new account number) with the company immediately. Bear in mind that it may be tough to get new credit during this ordeal if you don't do this now. Make sure you have at least two valid credit cards to show credit worthiness.

Banks and creditors may ask you to fill out and notarize their own fraud affidavits, a process that can become expensive. Use the Federal Trade Commission's standard affidavit (see the end of this book and make several copies.) So, unless the creditor offers to pay for a notary for their own affidavit, stick with the Federal Trade Commission Affidavit. If they balk, offer your bank's guaranteed signature. The Uniform Affidavit is sanctioned by the Federal Trade Commission (See Chapter 8 and available at **http://www.consumer.gov/idtheft**).

Step 3: Report the crime to police or the Secret Service, and the U. S. Postal Inspector by phone and in writing.

Within 24 hours of learning of the fraud, report the crime to the fraud unit of your local police or sheriff s department. Often the police in another county or state (where the fraud occurred) may not want to help you or even take a report, so at the very least call your local law enforcement. Give them as much documented evidence as possible, and in turn, make sure you get a copy of all police reports they file. Since there is a federal identity theft law, the Secret Service (or the FBI, Social Security Inspector or the U. S. Postal Inspector) may investigate (if there is a high dollar value or evidence of a fraud ring). If police in states other than your own won't help you, contact the Secret Service, which has jurisdiction for the crime crossing state lines. Remember, your local law enforcement has a duty to give you an informative report under most state laws. You must use it with the credit reporting agencies to delete the fraud from your profile. The police report must list in detail all the fraud information.

In dealing with law enforcement, make sure you:

- Remain very polite, no matter how frustrated you feel!
- Tell them the address where the credit cards (or credit lines) were sent. You will have learned this from the creditors or credit-reporting agencies.
- Make copies of all evidence you have gathered in your case and give it to them. This includes copies of all forged signatures, applications, addresses, and telephone numbers given for the fraudulent cards. Keep a copy of everything for yourself. Do not give copies of your credit report unless you block out your real account information. Your police report becomes public record, so instead list the fraud accounts on a separate page.
- Provide names and telephone numbers of all defrauded creditors so that the investigators can ask for records to aid the investigation. They also need to list each fraud account in the police report for your use with the credit-reporting agency.
- Insist that police file a report, even if it's only an "informational" report as opposed to an actual "crime" report. Some police departments are reluctant to write reports on such crimes. You

must understand that these cases are labor intensive and most law enforcement agencies don't have the resources to investigate and make it count for them. So be persistent! You will need a report. For example, credit card companies and banks will require you to show that report in order to verify the fraud and clear your name. Credit reporting agencies should block the fraud when they have it documented in a police report or report from the Secret Service. (Federal law requires the credit reporting agencies to block the fraud information if the report is specific.)

In fact, many creditors will not remove fraudulent information unless you file a police report and provide them the name of the fraud investigator and a copy of the police report, or at least the number of the report. Make sure the report lists all of the fraud accounts. You must file an addendum to the report if you learn of new fraud accounts.

So, don't let the police (or other law enforcement agencies or at least your Department of Motor Vehicles Fraud Division) turn you away without a report! Inform them of the federal law (18 USC 1028) and your own state laws (find those at **www.consumer.gov/idtheft**). If you need to, call or write to the chief of police, a city councilperson, the district attorney's office, or your local Victim Assistance Office. You may even need to call a state legislator or attorney general's office, or your governor's office. Do whatever's required to get that police report, because others to whom you're reporting the crime will need to see it before they'll take you seriously.

Understand also that because you placed fraud alerts on all your accounts, you may be the subject of suspicion by banks, and merchants that don't know you. To avoid delay and embarrassment, it's a good idea to carry a copy of the first page of your police report in your wallet at all times so you can prove you're not the imposter. Also, keep the phone number of the police fraud investigator handy and give it to creditors and others who require verification of your case.

You should also insist that the credit card companies, banks, department stores, and other "victims" who lost money call the police, cooperate with any investigation, and report the theft as well. They often are unwilling to help, since it is very time consuming and they have already lost money.

If a family member has impersonated you, and you choose not to file a police report, you'll be making the credit cleanup more difficult. It's still possible, however, to clear your name, if you follow all the other steps. You may be able to file a report with the Department of Motor Vehicles or another agency such as the Postal Inspector. (Mail fraud is usually part of these cases.) Even if you obtain a police report, often the police will not investigate if a family member did steal from you. You may consider having the relative admit the fraud (in writing), and offer to pay the fraud bills to the creditors. (Go to **www.idtheftcenter.org** for fact sheets on dealing with family members and fraud.)

Other necessary follow-up with police:

- Once a report is filed and an investigation begins, demand that the police fraud investigators give you copies of any evidence they have collected that has your name on it. They may say you have no right to that information because of privacy of the accused. However, you do have a right to anything with your name on it.

- Don't contact the impersonator yourself. Let the police handle it. Most impersonators are not violent, but it is wise not to confront these people. One victim, for instance, contacted her impersonator by phone, and subsequently she was "stalked" by this fraudster with numerous phone calls.

- Agree to cooperate if the district attorney or a federal prosecutor files a case. If there's enough evidence, the identity thief may agree to a plea bargain, which will eliminate your need to testify.
- If there is a plea bargain or conviction, you should write a letter (Victim Impact Statement) to the judge regarding the sentencing and to request monetary restitution as a victim.
- If you find you are a victim of Criminal Identity Theft, where someone uses your name and personal information while committing other crimes, you will need to clear your criminal record. Contact your local law enforcement to help clear your name in the other jurisdictions. You may need to contact the attorney general of your state.

Step 4: Write a description of your situation and complete the Uniform Affidavit.

As soon as you've figured out the basics of what's happened to you, complete the information affidavit explaining—who, what, where, when, and how (if you know). Give pertinent information about yourself and attach a utility bill (which may be required to prove your address), a government-issued identification, and the police report, too, once you receive it. Having this affidavit handy will save time because you won't need to repeat your story or re-write it to all the agencies that will need to hear it. Make numerous copies and put them in a file to send with letters. (See the Uniform Affidavit at the end of this book.)

Step 5: Reassert control of your bank accounts.

If you had checks stolen or bank accounts set up fraudulently, first report this to your bank, and then to the check-verification or check-guarantee companies.

When you pay by check, merchants often use one or the other of these kinds of firms to learn about your check-writing habits. A check-verification company provides an electronic database of people who've written bad checks or had their bank accounts closed because of bad checks. A check-guarantee company does the same and also promises to reimburse the retailer if the check bounces.

Not all of these companies will have a record of bad checks written in your name, and not all allow proactive fraud alerts. Federal law requires clocking of this fraud for a short time. So, it's important to contact each of the companies and explain your situation. They each have different requirements to follow to clear your name.

CheckRite	**(800) 766-2748**
ChexSystems	**(800) 428-9623**
Cross Check	**(800) 843-0760**
Equifax Check Services	**(800) 437-5120**
SCAN	**(800) 262-7771**
TeleCheck	**(800) 366-2425**

The databases of the check guarantee/verification services sometimes contain errors. You might, for example, be listed as a bad-check writer by mistake, or someone could be using your driver's license number or checking account number to pass bad checks. In either case, you have a right to have the error corrected.

If you write a check and have it declined by the merchant, ask for the name, phone number, and address of the check guarantee or verification service that rejected your check and obtain copies of the fraudulent checks. Then call them to find out what information they have about you in their files and, if necessary, how to correct erroneous information.

If you suspect fraudulent use of your own checks, you'll also need to:

- Put stop-payments on any outstanding checks that you're unsure of. If your checks are stolen, you should not only report that to the check-verification companies, but also immediately contact your bank, stop payment on all the checks, and close the account. When opening new accounts, put only your initials and last name on the account. Do not pre-print your Social Security number, driver's license, or phone number on the check. Never write your Social Security number on the check. If you live in a state that uses the Social Security number for your driver's license number, change the number.
- Put a new password (not your mother's maiden name) and a fraud alert on any old or new accounts. But open new accounts only if the current accounts have been affected by the fraud.
- Cancel those checking and savings accounts that have been affected by fraud. Obtain new account numbers and give the bank a secret password for these new accounts. (Never use your mother's maiden name because that's on your birth certificate, which is a public record easily available. Also, avoid using children's or a pet's name, because those may be well known to other people.)
- Tell the bank that your password is required for use before any action can be taken on the account — deposits, withdrawals, name change, address change, billing information, and so on (follow this up in writing).

- Call and write to your true non-fraudulent accounts and notify them of the fraud situation and place a fraud alert. Also, for accounts that haven't been fraudulently invaded, change your password.

Step 6: Don't pay fraudulent bills.

Don't pay any bills that are not yours, even if you think it's going to make your life easier. When you acquiesce, it's as if you're admitting that the bill is yours—don't do it! Similarly, never cover any fraudulent checks. Never file bankruptcy due to fraud!

If collection companies continue to harass you after you have written letters, inform them that they're violating the law and keep documentation so you may take legal action if they persist.

Step 7: Get a new ATM Card without the VISA or MasterCard logo.

If your ATM or debit card has been stolen or compromised, get a new one, including a new account and password. Do not continue to use your old password.

When creating a PIN for your new card, don't use common numbers like your address, the last four digits of your Social Security number or your birth date. Again, those are too obvious.

Ask your bank for a card that does not have the Visa or MasterCard logo. ATM cards with credit card logos are dangerous. Charges made come directly out of your checking account and federal law does not protect you in the same way that it does when you have a regular credit card, which lets you dispute questionable charges before payment, if fraud occurs. With the ATM Visa or MasterCard you must prove fraud, and it may take months to get your money back if you ever do! With a regular ATM card, you can still obtain cash or make a deposit at any ATM and use it as a check guarantee card.

Step 8: Straighten out your mail.

Mail theft is a felony. Notify the local U.S. Postal Inspector if you suspect an identity thief has filed a change of address form in your name with the post office or has used the mail to commit credit or bank fraud.

Call and write to the postal authority in the city where the fraud was committed (i.e., the address to which fraudulent credit cards were sent), and ask for a criminal investigation. Your local postmaster can give you names, addresses, and telephone numbers of postal authorities there. Ask for a fraud complaint form to complete to make sure no mail with your name on it continues to be sent to the fraudulent address.

Step 9: Alert your public utilities.

Call your telephone, electrical, gas, trash, and water utilities and ask for a password. Warn them of the possibility that someone may attempt to open new service using your identification. Give them a password that will be required before any account changes will be made. If the impersonator has opened accounts in your name, cancel the accounts due to fraud, and place a fraud alert!

Step 10: Contact the Secret Service or FBI if the fraud occurs out of state.

The Secret Service has jurisdiction over financial fraud, but it usually doesn't investigate individual cases unless the dollar amount is very high or you are among the victims of a fraud ring. The Secret Service's interest is not in small individual crime, but in organized groups that may be committing identity theft.

That's especially true if such thefts extend across county, state, or national boundaries and, thus, are beyond the reach of the local authorities.

So, keep in mind that the Secret Service is mainly interested in seeing if the information you report fits into a larger picture. The agency is probably not going to investigate your individual crime.

However, to further interest the Secret Service in your case, you may want to ask the fraud department of the credit card companies and / or banks, as well as the police fraud investigator, to notify the particular Secret Service agent they work with and possibly the local Identity Theft Task Force.

Step 11: Notify Social Security and taxing authorities.

Call or write the Social Security Administration to report fraudulent use of your Social Security number. Don't expect much help here, though; there's little the Social Security Administration can do. The Social Security Inspector General's Office will collaborate with the Secret Service and Identity Theft Task Forces on large cases of mail fraud, computer hacking, etc. (See our resources list in Chapter Eight).

Even though the identity thief may have used your Social Security number, don't change it! That will only make you look more suspicious to future creditors. Your new number will be linked to your credit report along with the old numbers and that may cause delays in obtaining new credit.

Getting a new Social Security number will also cause confusion with all earlier records, such as those pertaining to your health, education, legal status, and finances. Thus, canceling your old number and requesting a new one may be a "cure" that's worse than the "disease"!

Request your Personal Earnings and Benefit Estimate Statement (PEBES) from the Social Security Administration to make sure that the impersonator hasn't been using your Social Security number for his or her earnings. The IRS could tax you for earnings that aren't yours.

Order your Personal Earnings and Benefit Estimate Statement by calling: (800) 772-1213. You may write to them as well. (See the address the resources list in Chapter Eight.)

Step 12: Check on your passport.

If you have a passport, notify the passport office in writing to be on the lookout for anyone ordering a new passport under your name. There have been cases of impersonators committing crimes in other countries with fraudulently obtained passports. Terrorists use fraudulent passports as well.

Tell the passport office not to issue a new passport with a change of name or address without verification in writing from you. Ask them to place a fraud alert on your file. Along with your correspondence, send a copy of the key pages of your current passport.

If you don't have a passport, you may wish to apply for one to establish a further form of identification, and to block your impostor from getting one in your name. Check the government pages of your phone book for the number of your nearest passport office, or go to your local post office for information. (**www.travelstate.gov / passport-services.html**)

Another good number to know: Federal Government Information Center: (800) 688-9889 for help in obtaining government agency phone numbers.

Step 13: Protect your phone, phone card, and cell phone.

If your long-distance calling card or cell phone has been stolen or you discover fraudulent charges on your bill, cancel the account and open a new one. Provide a password, which must be used whenever the account is changed. You are entitled to request in writing all evidence of the fraud from these companies as well.

Step 14: Change your driver's license number if used by fraudster.

If someone is using your driver's license as identification on bad checks, you'll need to go to the local office of your state department of motor vehicles to request a new number.

If an impersonator is using your driver's license number, you should get a new license and cancel the old one. Don't cancel your driver's license number until the motor vehicles department verifies that a new card with your name and number was issued to an imposter at a different address.

You should also:

- Call the state to see if another license was issued in your name.
- Put a fraud alert on your license.
- Fill out your state's department of vehicle licensing fraud complaint form to begin a fraud investigation. Send supporting documents with the completed form to the nearest motor vehicles department investigation office.
- Tell the department in writing not to issue a new driver's license without your verification of a change of address or name.

- Be aware that the impersonator can easily purchase a fake driver's license for a small fee from another criminal. The department of motor vehicle licensing has no jurisdiction over such a fraudulently manufactured license. If you suspect that such a license was produced with your name and the impersonator's picture, let the DMV know.
- Get a copy of your driving record to see if there have been any traffic violations or accidents involving the impersonator. If there are, write to the vehicle licensing department and request that they be removed from your record. Get a copy of any court records and police reports.
- Find out if a picture or a fingerprint was taken of the imposter when he or she came to the department's offices. If so, get copies of the documents and give them to the police, or ask law enforcement to get these documents.

Step 15: Contact your auto, health, life, or business insurer, if necessary.

If your driver's license is misused, you'll also need to notify your auto insurance company that someone may be using your name while driving a car. This will help protect you if the impersonator has an accident or commits a moving violation. Sometimes an imposter will use your health insurance or business insurance, or even buy a life insurance policy in your name making the impostor the beneficiary (with his real name)!

Step 16: Clear your name in the courts—civil and criminal.

Sometimes, identity-theft victims become the object of civil actions brought on by the impersonator. Even worse, victims sometimes are wrongfully accused of crimes committed by the imposter.

James was an investment manager of $100 million in client accounts for one of the nation's largest and most respected mutual fund companies. When James' Pennsylvania insurance license came up for renewal, the company ran a routine background check and discovered a shocking revelation: James was a convicted felon who had pleaded guilty to loan and credit card fraud. So the company immediately fired him. James insisted that he had never been arrested, much less convicted of any crime. But the company forced him to leave the building immediately, without returning to his office to gather his belongings. The truth was the real James was truly innocent.

Here's what to do to clear your name:

Civil judgments:

If a civil judgment (i.e. involving a legal action by a credit card company) has been entered in your name because of something done by the imposter, contact the court where the judgment was entered and get the name, phone number, and address of the attorney who filed the case against you. Call the attorney for the company (Plaintiff in the lawsuit) and report that you are a victim of identity theft. Then find out what you need to do to expunge the judgment and record.

You may discover civil judgments on your credit report (e.g., a bankruptcy) or you may learn that there have been attempts to attach your bank accounts or put a lien on your property.

For civil judgments, call the court in which the civil judgment was filed and find out how to get a copy of the entire court file. Write and request the file be sent to you. There will be a fee for that. Call the attorney(s) involved in the case. (Their names will be in the file.)

False criminal judgments and criminal prosecutions: You could be wrongfully named in a criminal complaint. That could happen if the government charges the imposter with a crime he committed while using your name . . . or worse yet, charges you for a crime he committed in your name. In either case, it's serious business, and you'll need to clear your name.

Contact your local police and provide all documentation of the fraud. Have them help you contact the police in the jurisdiction where the perpetrator was arrested and / or convicted. You should also contact the attorney general of your state to find out the specific record. Some states, like California, have set up a system for a victim to go to court to get a certificate of Identity Theft (and clearance) and may register your name with the Department of Justice to protect you. In some courts you will need to have a criminal law attorney, who is familiar with identity theft, to help you. If you don't know one, ask the local bar association for a referral. If you do not have the funds, ask the court to provide you a public defender.

If your files are complete and organized, with evidence, you can expedite the clearing of your name—but it must be in writing.

Remember, a false criminal charge against you is potentially a very serious problem, perhaps a worst-case scenario of identity theft. In addition to getting a lawyer, you may need to contact the Federal Department of Justice, or the FBI to assist you in clearing your name from the National Criminal Databases.

If you find civil judgments on your credit reports or you learn of criminal records with your name, it's a good idea to do a background check on yourself to look for other civil actions or criminal records against you.

If law enforcement won't do a background check, you may wish to do your own. There are web sites that do this for a fee, such as **www.knowx.com**, **www.docusearch.com**, **www.ussearch.com**, **www.mybackgroundcheck.com**, and others. You may wish to look for a certified private investigator in your area.

Step 17: Consider getting legal help to restore your credit or take legal action against negligent agencies.

As you know, the burden is on you—and there's a limit to what an attorney can do that you can't do yourself in terms of cleaning up the financial mess. However, you will need legal representation if you intend to file a suit to seek damages for your losses against companies that were violating laws, which caused you loss.

If yours is a complex case involving very large amounts of money and/or you run into difficulty clearing up your credit history, you should consult a consumer-law attorney. A lawyer could help you decide whether to sue creditors and/or credit bureaus if they're not cooperating in removing fraudulent entries from your credit report, or if you think their negligence led to your problem. Make sure you see an attorney who is familiar with the Fair Credit Report Act and identity theft, your state laws, as well as other federal laws.

There are strict time guidelines as to when you must bring action for negligence. There are also strict deadlines under the Fair Credit Reporting Act. Federal law now says a victim must bring an action within two years from the date of discovery, but no later than five years from the violation (regardless of the discovery.) So carefully review the inquiry section of all three of your credit reports. Look for the companies that may have inquired about your credit as a result of an impersonator's request for credit. Find the dates of that first fraudulent inquiry. If your credit mess isn't cleared after sending the letters in this booklet, seek out an attorney to review your case immediately. Write the date you first learned of the fraud. Also determine the date of the first violation. It must be within the last five (5) years.

Unfortunately, many victims do not even discover the fraud for over a year or more. Get legal advice for yourself based on your situation as quickly as possible.

I am not encouraging you to sue, but I am telling you to get legal advice and find out the legal options available for your specific case.

Before you make an appointment to see a lawyer, make sure that your expense logs and letters are in order, and that you have made copies of everything to bring with you to the first appointment.

Step 18: Get a handle on the stress.

Know, for starters, that you are not alone. Many others have gone through this, or are going through it now. The Federal Trade Commission's study found that there are about 10 million new victims each year. Many victims believe that psychological counseling is helpful to deal with this stress and anxiety.

Try to use your anger and emotional response effectively. Don't get angry and yell at customer-service representatives, advocates, or government workers. Even when frustrated, try to stay calm so you will get the kind of help that you need and win the person's sympathy and assistance.

Remember: Even if a company facilitated the fraud or the government agency is being balky, the person you're talking to is not personally at fault. You're angry at the situation, not the people whom you need to help you resolve it. So try to separate the person from the problem. This is critical!

In any event, don't think you're going crazy. It's common to have strong emotional reactions, such as crying and feeling despondent, angry, or agitated. Many people victimized by this crime experience emotional and physical distress, and even Post Traumatic Stress Disorder. Go to **www.idtheftcenter.org** and look at their fact sheets on this issue. There, you may join a support group, or even start one in your own area.

Step 19: Seek changes in the law.

Use the energy that stems from your anger to motivate you to help solve the problem. Your experience will almost certainly have made you sensitive to the fact that there are few effective laws to prevent identity theft. The United States Public Interest Research Group (**www.uspirg.org**) provides lobbying to promote your rights as identity theft victims. You may join them.

When you have your situation under control, begin to broaden your concern into the privacy and identity plights of yourself and others. Join others in demanding policy changes in the institutions that make the crime of identity theft so easy!

Write to your state and federal legislators, and to the editor of your local newspaper. Demand stronger privacy protection and fraud assistance by creditors and credit bureaus.

Make complaints to The Federal Trade Commission (877) IDTHEFT, or visit the FTC Identity Theft Complaint Center at **www.consumer.gov/idtheft**.

Step 20: Don't give in, don't give up!

Perhaps the most important thing to do is persist. Don't lose heart! Be prepared for a long-distance run, not a quick sprint. In short, if you're like most identity-fraud victims, you've already experienced fear, frustration, and exhaustion.

The most important thing to remember is that phone calls are not enough—a company can say they have no record of your call—so always confirm all conversations in writing. Our book *From Victim to Victor: A Step-By-Step Guide For Ending the Nightmare of Identity Theft* (Second Edition) has all the attorney-composed letters pre-written on CD—the law and your legal rights are included in the letters. All you do is put the CD in your computer (for a PC or Mac) and pull up the file, complete with your information to save you some effort and costs of using an attorney on an hourly basis. For more information go to **www.identitytheft.org**, call (800) 725-0807, or visit **www.amazon.com**. To protect your rights, make sure you are specific as to your legal demands. If you wish, you may consult with a lawyer and review the Fair Credit Reporting Act—and possible violations relating to your situation.

Chapter Seven

Where To From Here?

"Many are the uses of adversity,"

—Shakespeare

We can use all the adversity of this crime as a springboard to make important privacy changes in our society. Now that you better understand this epidemic of identity theft, we hope you'll become more careful, more privacy conscious, more aware of how vulnerable you are, yet confident that you can handle whatever comes your way, if you are diligent.

Having read this far, you might feel that the task of safeguarding your identity is a daunting one. Indeed it is, since so much of your information is passing through the hands of others and disseminated in databases without your knowledge, and far beyond your control. We, as a society, can create solutions, but only when all the players become actively involved in a concerted effort. This book gives you a formula for significantly reducing the crime of identity theft—since we doubt we will ever eradicate it.

As you've learned here, you can take many steps to prevent key pieces of personal identification from getting into the hands of imposters. Proper disposal of your paper-based information through shredding is an important first step. Ordering your credit reports twice a year or getting a credit monitoring service is another. The latter is not a prevention step per se, but it allows you to discover identity theft early and minimize the impact on your financial health. Chapters Two, Three, and Four list scores of such steps to reduce your risk—consider incorporating these suggestions one page at a time.

Likewise, if you work in business, a government agency, or a nonprofit organization, you can be extra cautious yourself, and can encourage your employer to adopt responsible information-handling practices in the workplace, in order to protect personal information from getting into the wrong hands. Chapter Four gives you many tips to implement a strategy in the workplace, but you can't be expected to operate in a vacuum. We must all advocate for structural and philosophical changes in commerce, the credit industry, with laws and practices, and in the criminal justice system's approach to identity theft and privacy protection.

In 1998, the federal Identity Theft and Assumption Deterrence Act was passed by the U. S. Congress and signed into law. It made identity theft a federal felony offense. In 2004, Congress passed the Identity Theft Penalty Enhancement Act, extending maximum jail time from three to five years for some identity theft, and creating 25-year sentences for aggravated identity theft related to terrorism. While the passage of these federal criminal laws was a major step forward, more stringent criminal and protection laws still must be enacted at the state level, since that's where most cases are reported. With regard to the prosecution of the criminals, the Secret Service and FBI have jurisdiction over this federal crime, but they do not have the resources to deal with individual theft and problems at the local level unless it is a connected to a national crime ring, great dollar loss, or involves terrorism.

Criminal laws are of little use unless they are enforced. Since identity theft is such an easy crime to commit, and so complex to investigate, local and federal agencies must be very selective about which cases they investigate. Even at the local level, law enforcement usually won't investigate unless the victim suffers an extremely high monetary loss. Policing agencies must be adequately funded at the local level to investigate more identity theft cases and bring perpetrators to justice. Prosecutors must seek stiff penalties for identity thieves, and judges must take this crime seriously. We've seen many cases in which perpetrators are given probation or community service because the crime is considered nonviolent. The growing legion of identity theft victims can attest to the crime's harmful impact on their lives, regardless of the absence of physical violence. Monetary reimbursement for victims must also be sought through restitution. But, we must remember that law enforcement can only react to a criminal situation. It is the financial industry that can be pro-active to prevent the crime.

We must push for better federal and state laws and business practices that protect and limit the uncontrolled dissemination of our unique identifiers like the Social Security number, and our biometric information (like fingerprints, facial scans), which will be used much more frequently in the near future. As long as this type of information, and other susceptible data is bought, sold, and transferred without restrictive safeguards, criminals will find this kind of fraud very easy.

Although the Fair Credit Reporting Act (15 USC Section 1681 et seq.) was amended by Congress in 2003 to include the Fair and Accurate Credit Transactions Act to institute better procedures to protect consumer privacy and assist victims of identity theft, there is still not adequate accountability in commerce and government to require agencies and government to protect your sensitive information and your privacy.

Here are a few of the guidelines we suggest:

- The credit granting industry must adopt better methods of determining the true identity of credit applicants before issuing credit, and they should verify address discrepancies with a phone call or letter before extending credit. This is especially important for instant credit applications, favored by identity thieves because of minimal verification procedures. Convenience checks (those that you receive from your credit card company that may be easily forged by a fraudster) should be illegal to send unless you specifically request them from the company.
- There should be significant financial penalties for credit grantors who are clearly negligent, in failing to properly discard information or in extending credit to imposters. Presently, federal law prohibits an individual victim from bringing a cause of action against a company for many violations of the Fair and Accurate Credit Transactions Act. In fact, even the attorney general of your state is precluded from bringing actions to protect your rights. The Federal Trade Commission is the authority that has the jurisdiction to file a lawsuit—and that agency cannot represent individuals. The FTC can only investigate and file a legal action if there are thousands of people harmed by a particular company. Often, individual victims who are harmed by companies are frustrated because they can't get legal redress from the companies who facilitated the crime.
- Any company or governmental agency that learns of a security breach online or off-line of any sensitive information should be required to notify all potential victims, and institute and adhere to best practices for information handling.
- Your information should not be sold or transferred without

your prior permission. Federal law allows the financial industry to sell and transfer your information unless you opt out. This is very exhausting for you, since it requires calling or writing myriad companies and asking them not to sell or share your information with third parties. Additionally, federal law (The Financial Modernization Act of 1999) also allows financial companies to share with affiliates without allowing you to "opt out." These laws give you little control over how your personal information is used. California and North Dakota have enacted laws that require the financial industry to get permission from customers (opt-in) before sharing or selling information to third parties, and California requires companies to permit "opt out" of sharing their information with affiliated companies. All Americans should have the control to limit the dissemination of their sensitive data. Therefore, federal law should change to protect the privacy of all citizens, by requiring companies to get your permission first before sharing your personal profile.

- Since the credit reporting industry is in a unique position to detect financial identity theft at its inception, they should have a duty to take extra precautions. Credit bureaus (Equifax, Experian, and Trans Union) can and should alert potential victims, credit grantors, and authorities when suspicious inquiries are made before extensive damage is done. Credit reporting laws must be strengthened to give victims meaningful redress (i.e. allow for class actions) when the carelessness of credit bureaus is a factor in impeding the victim's ability to regain his creditworthiness. Such laws also need to give consumers more control over the distribution of their credit reports, enabling those consumers who so desire to take their credit reports "off-line," by allowing anyone in any state to "freeze" his/her file with a password and to unfreeze it only when applying for credit. Only a few states have passed laws to allow this protection.

- The financial industry, the healthcare industry, companies, and government agencies who collect, use, transfer and share our sensitive data must maintain our information securely, and must be held legally responsible when their faulty procedures facilitate fraud and identity theft.

Government and private industry must develop workable, trustworthy procedures for securing our information. With the high concern for homeland security and the danger of terrorism, our government is trying to deal with the delicate balance between the need to collect and share sensitive information and critical privacy issues. You will see a greater push to obtain your fingerprints, iris scans, retina and facial scans, and perhaps even your DNA. Even more intrusive measures are being suggested, such as implanting computer chips in your body to identify you, and provide extensive facts about your life. These chips are already being implanted in people. Some are for health reasons, some as a precaution for kidnapping. The possibility of detrimental secondary uses of these chips and biometric identifiers must be explored and resolved before we implement their standard use.

As a society, we've seen how identity theft has reached sweeping proportions as a result of our lack of privacy—meaning the loss of control over how our personal information is used without our knowledge. The technology of the information age and instantaneous transfer of data has transformed our lives in many wonderful ways, but it also has created insidious, new crimes and has eroded our privacy. Before it is too late, we must institute measures to preserve some level of control over our private lives. Governmental agencies and private companies need to institute secure, trustworthy procedures to ensure the safekeeping of all of our personal information. The following list of fair information principles is adapted from policies developed some years ago by the Organization for Economic Cooperation and Development. These have formed the basis of many of our privacy laws and business practices, and must be instituted globally to protect us in the information age.

We believe that identity theft and the disastrous effects on victims and our culture would be radically reduced if government agencies and all of commerce would implement these eight steps:

1. **Provide open policies.**
   There should be an open, written clarification about exactly what personal information is to be collected. The existence and nature of personal data held by the organization should be readily available for inspection by individuals.

2. **Designate specific purpose or use.**
   The customer or citizen (if governmental) should be told why the information is being collected at the time it is gathered. There should be no other use of that data without your consent.

3. **Describe data collection limitations.**
   The information collected should be limited to the information necessary for the stated purpose and nothing more. Information shouldn't be collected simply because it may be useful in the future.

4. **Limit use and transfer of data.**
   The information collected should be limited to the use of the business or organization that collected it. The information shouldn't be revealed or sold to others without <u>prior</u> consent from the individual or legal authority.

5. **Provide consumer inspection.**

The individual should have a right to consent, inspect, and correct (and delete if appropriate) his or her personal information.

6. **Institute quality controls.**
   The information should be accurate, complete, timely, and relevant to the purpose for which it is to be used. Whenever possible, the information should be collected directly from the individual, not from third party information brokers.

7. **Develop strict security measures.**
   There should be reasonable security safeguards against risks such as loss, unauthorized access, destruction, or alteration. Only those with a need to know should have access.

8. **Implement standards of accountability, enforcement, and redress.**
   The business or governmental agency must be held accountable to the individuals. There should be enforcement mechanisms that provide remedies to those harmed by the lack of accountability. Privacy audits should be conducted regularly, as should employee-training programs. Sanctions should be applied for employees, companies, or agencies that violate these policies or standards.

This book has given you many tools, tips, and resources to Safeguard Your Identity and Protect Yourself With a Personal Privacy Audit for your home and workplace. Although privacy and identity theft challenges won't be resolved by you alone, as an individual you can make a tremendous difference in your life and in the lives of those you deal with each day. Now that you are aware of actions you can take, and what you should expect from others in a position to protect you, please make your voice heard regarding your privacy concerns. Educate your employer, doctor, friends, business associates, and especially your government representatives with positive suggestions such as we've shared with you. Write letters to the editor, and apprize others of what must be done to ensure our privacy and security. We welcome your ideas and suggestions for how we all may create solutions to protect our privacy and identity. You'll find information on how to contact us on the About the Author page in the back of this book. Together, we as conscientious citizens can collaborate to accomplish great changes to protect our privacy—the key to preserving our freedom and democracy.

> *Throughout history, it has been the inaction of those who could have acted; the indifference of those who should have known better; the silence of the voice of justice when it mattered most; that has made it possible for evil to triumph.*

—Haile Selassi
111th Emperor of Ethiopia (1892-1975)

Chapter Eight

Resources to Assist You

Identity Theft And Privacy Protection

- CALPIRG (California Public Interest Research Group)
  Research and lobbying consumer group that addresses issues of identity theft and consumer issues.
  1107 9th St., Suite 601
  Sacramento, CA 95814
  Phone: (916) 448-4516
  E-mail: info@calpirg.org
  Web: **www.calpirg.org**

- **Center for Democracy and Technology**
  The goal of this organization is to bring democracy to the Internet.
  1634 "I" Street NW, Suite 1100
  Washington, D.C. 20006
  Phone: (202) 637-9800
  Fax: (202) 637-0968
  E-mail: feedback@cdt.org
  Web: **www.cdt.org**

- **Computer Professionals for Social Responsibility**
  Provides policy makers with realistic assessments of power, promise and problems of information technology.
  P. O. Box 717
  Palo Alto, CA 94302
  Phone: (650) 322-3778
  E-mail cpsr@cpsr.org
  Web: **www.cpsr.org**

- **Consumer Action Credit and Finance Project**
  Provides publications on secured credit.
  717 Market Street, Suite 310
  San Francisco, CA 94103
  Phone: (415) 777-9635 – complaint hot line
  Phone: (415) 255-3879 – publication orders
  Web: **http://www.consumer-action.org**

- **Consumer Federation of America**
  Association of 240 pro-consumer groups whose aim is to advance consumer interest through advocacy and education.
  1424 16th St. NW, Suite 604
  Washington, D.C. 20036
  Phone: (202) 387-6121
  Web: **http://www.consumerfed.org/**

- **Consumers Union**
  Publishes Consumer Reports magazine and also acts as an advocacy office for consumer legislation.
  1666 Connecticut Ave. NW, Suite 310
  Washington, D.C. 20009-1039
  Phone: (202) 462-6262
  Web: **http://www.consumersunion.org**

- **Electronic Privacy Information Center**
  Monitors federal legislation and encryption policy pertaining to freedom of expression issues on the Internet.
  1718 Connecticut Ave. NW
  Washington, D.C. 20009
  Phone: (202) 483-1140
  Fax: (202) 483-1248
  E-mail: info@epic.org
  Web: **www.epic.org**

- **Identity Theft Prevention and Survival**
  Provides assistance to consumers and identity theft victims with resources, books, and legal assistance.
  Mari J. Frank, Esq.
  28202 Cabot Road, Suite 300
  Laguna Niguel, CA 92677
  Phone: (800) 725-0807 or (949) 364-1511
  Fax: (949) 363-7561
  E-mail: contact@identitytheft.org
  Web: **www.identitytheft.org**

- **Identity Theft Resource Center**
  Provides support and assistance to victims of identity theft.
  Co-Directors: Linda Goldman-Foley, Jay Foley
  P.O.Box 26833
  San Diego, CA. 92196
  Phone: (858) 693-7935
  e-mail: itrc@idtheftcenter.org
  Web: **http://idtheftcenter.org**

- **Junkbusters Corp.**
  Provides self-defense against privacy-invading marketing
  P.O. Box 7034
  Green Brook, NJ 08812

Phone: (908) 753-7861
Web: **Junkbusters.com**
Please do not send requests to be removed from marketing lists to this address.
Junkbusters only operates online. Requests may be mailed to the Direct Marketing Association.

- **National Organization for Victim Assistance (NOVA)**
  Refers victims of crime to local victim assistance programs.
  1730 Park Rd., NW
  Washington, D.C. 20010
  Phone: (202) 232-6682 Hotline: (800) 879-6682
  Web: **http://www.trynova.org**

- **National Center for Victims of Crime**
  Refers victims of crime to local services. Provides counseling and victim services. Publishes bulletins on various criminal topics.
  2000 M. St. NW, Suite 480
  Washington, D.C. 20036
  Phone: (800) FYI-CALL or (202) 467-8700
  Web: **www.ncvc.org**

- **Office of Privacy Protection-California**
  Provides information for consumers and victims regarding California and Federal Law.
  400 "R" Street, Suite 3080
  Sacramento, CA 95814
  Phone: (866)785-9663
  (916) 323-0637
  Web: **http://www.privacy.ca.gov**

- **Privacy Rights Clearinghouse**
  A non-profit consumer information, privacy protection, and advocacy program.

Beth Givens, Director
3100 5th Ave. Suite B
San Diego, CA 92103
Phone: (619) 298-3396
Fax: (619) 298-5681
Web: **www.privacyrights.org**

- **The Foundation For Taxpayer and Consumer Rights**
  Non-profit organization to support consumer rights.
  1750 Ocean Park Blvd., Suite 200
  Santa Monica, CA 90405
  Phone: (310) 392-0522
  Fax: (310) 392-8874
  E-mail: consumerwatchdog@consumerwatchdog.org
  Web: **http://www.consumerwatchdog.org**

- **U. S. PIRG**
  U. S. Public Interest Research Group, the national lobbying office for state PIRGs.
  Edmund Mierzwinski, Director
  218 "D" St., SE
  Washington, D.C. 20003
  Phone: (202) 546-9707
  E-mail: uspirg@pirg.org
  Web: **www.pirg.org**

Legal Resources

Contact your State Bar Association or your local Bar Association for the names of consumer-law attorneys. You may also wish to contact:

- **Center for Law in the Public Interest**
  Non profit law firm that specializes in public interest litigation

and counseling on public policy.
3250 Ocean Park Blvd., Suite 300
Santa Monica, CA 90405
Phone: (310) 314-1947
Fax: (310) 314-1957
E-mail: information@clipi.org
Web: **http://www.clipi.org/**

- **National Association of Consumer Advocates**
  1730 Rhode Island NW, Suite 805
  Washington, D.C. 20036
  Phone: (202) 452-1989
  Fax: (202) 452-0099
  E-mail: info@naca.net
  Web: **www.naca.net**

- **National Consumer Law Center, Inc.**
  Provides case assistance and legal research. Provides representation for low income and community based organizations.
  77 Summer St., 10th Floor
  Boston, MA 02110-1006
  Phone: (617) 542-8010
  Fax: (617) 542-8028
  E-mail: consumerlaw@nclc.org

- **FBI**
  Criminal Justice Information Services Division
  J. Edgar Hoover Building
  935 Pennsylvania Avenue, NW
  Washington, D.C. 20535-0001
  Phone: (202) 324-3000
  Web: **http://www.fbi.gov/**
  National Fraud Info Hotline: (800) 876-7060
  If someone has committed a crime using your identity, write to

the FBI and ask for your criminal history (include your finger-prints and a check for $18.00). Explain that you are a victim of identity theft.
IFCC (Internet Fraud Complaint Center) FBI
Web: www.ifccfbi.gov

- **National Association of Attorneys General**
  Consumer Protection and Charities Counsel
  750 First Street, N.E. Suite 1100
  Washington, D.C. 20002
  Phone: (202) 326-6000
  Fax: (202) 408-7014
  Web: **http://www.naag.org**

- **U.S. Department of Justice, Identity Theft Information**
  Web: **www.usdoj.gov/criminal/fraud/idtheft.html**

Credit Card Companies

- **American Express**
  (800) 528-2122
  Web: **http://www.americanexpress.com**

- **MasterCard Global Service Center**
  Phone: (800) 307-7309
  Web: **http://www.mastercard.com**

- **Visa Assistance Center**
  Phone: (800) VISA911 (Hotline)
  Web: http://www.visa.com

Credit Reporting Bureaus

To order one free annual credit report from each of the three credit reporting agencies, call 877-322-8228, *or visit* ***www.annualcreditreport.com.*** *When you call to report fraud, you will get a voice mail and must provide your Social Security number. Use your cell phone number or home number as the number to call if creditors wish to check if you requested credit.*

- **Equifax**
  To report fraud: (800) 525-6285
  P.O. Box 740241
  Atlanta, GA 30374-0241
  To order copy of report: (800) 685-1111
  P.O. Box 740241
  Atlanta, GA 30374-0241
  Web: **www.equifax.com**
  To opt out of pre-approved offers of credit for all three credit bureaus call:
  (888) 5 OPTOUT [(888) 567-8688]

- **Experian (formerly TRW)**
  To report fraud: (888) 397-3742
  Experian Consumer Fraud Assistance
  P.O. Box 9532
  Allen, TX 75013
  To order copy of report: (888) 397-3742
  P.O. Box 9532
  Allen, TX 75013
  Web: **www.experian.com**

- **TransUnion**
  To report fraud: (800) 680-7289
  Fraud Victim Assistance Division
  P.O. Box 6790

Fullerton, CA 92834-6790
To order copy of report: (800) 888-4213
P.O. Box 6790
Fullerton, CA 92834-6790
Web: **www.transunion.com**

Check-Verification / Check-Guarantee Firms

- **Global Payments: (800) 766-2748**
- **ChexSystems: (800) 428-9623**
- **Cross Check: (800) 843-0760**
- **Certigy Equifax Check Services: (800) 437-5120**
- **SCAN: (800) 262-7771**
- **TeleCheck: (800) 710-9898**
- **International Check Services: (800) 526-5380**

Data Compilers

To remove your name from lists that companies rent and sell, write or call the following companies:

Mail Preference Service
Direct Marketing Association
P.O. Box 643
Carmel, NY 10512-0643
Web: **www.dmaconsumers.org**

- **Federal Trade Commission Do Not Call Registry**
  1-888-382-1222
  (Must call from the phone number that you wish to register)
  Web: **www.donotcall.gov**

- **First Data Info-Source Donnelley Marketing, Inc.**
  Data Base Operations
  416 S. Bell
  Aims, IA 50010
  (888) 633-4402

Other Groups And Governmental Agencies

- **Comptroller of the Currency**
  Administrator of National Banks
  Customer Assistance Group
  1301 McKinney Street, Suite 3450
  Houston, TX 77010-9050
  Phone: (800) 613-6743
  Fax: (713) 336-4301
  Web: **http://www.occ.treas.gov**

- **Federal Citizen Information Center**
  Referral to appropriate agency
  (800) 688-9889 (800) 333-4636

- **The Federal Trade Commission Identity Theft Clearinghouse**
  The Consumer Protection Mission of the FTC is to protect consumers from companies that misinform or overreach with regard to our economy.
  Identity Theft Clearinghouse
  600 Pennsylvania Ave., NW
  Washington, D.C. 20580
  (877) IDTHEFT (438-4338)
  Web: **http://www.consumer.gov/idtheft**

- **Internal Revenue Service**
  Office of the Privacy Advocate

Room 7050 OS:PA
1111 Constitution Ave., NW
Washington, D. C. 20224
Fraud: (800) 829-0433
Taxpayer Advocates Office:
(877) 777-4778
Web: **http://www.treas.gov/irs/ci**
www.irs.gov

- **National Fraud Information Center**
  Consumer Assistance Service
  Web: **www.fraud.org**
  (800) 876-7060 – help line for victims of fraud

- **U. S. Postal Inspection Service**
  475 L'Enfant Plaza West, SW
  Room 3100
  Washington, D.C. 20260-1000
  (202) 268-4396
  Web: **http://www.usps.com/postalinspectors/**

- **Private Citizen, Inc**
  Provides information and assistance on how to get rid of junk mailers and junk callers.
  P. O. Box 233
  Naperville, IL 60566
  (800) CUT-JUNK (288-5865)
  (630) 393-2370
  Email: pci@private-citizen.com
  Web: **http://www.privatecitizen.com**

- **Privacy International**
  A public interest research group that deals with privacy issues

at the national and international level.
1718 Connecticut Avenue, NW, Suite 200
Washington, D.C. 20009
(202) 483-1217
Email: privacyint@privacy.org
Web: **http://www.privacyinternational.org/**

- **Social Security Administration**
  Office of Inspector General
  Social Security Administration
  Office of Communications
  Suite 300 Altmeyer Building
  6401 Security Blvd
  Baltimore, MD 21235
  To report Fraud: (800) 269-0271
  P.O. Box 17768
  Baltimore, MD 21235

  To order Personal Earnings and Benefits Statement:
  (800) 772-1213
  Office of Inspector General: (800) 269-0271
  Web:
  www.ssa.gov/org/publicfraudreporting/index.htm
  www.ssa.gov/oig/guidelin.htm

- **US Department of State Passport Services**
  Consular Lost/Stolen Passport Section
  1111 19th Street, NW, Suite 500
  Washington, D.C. 20036
  (202) 955-0430
  Web: **http://www.travel.state.gov/passport/lost.htmll**

- **Federal Deposit Insurance Corporation (FDIC)**
  Supervises state-chartered banks that are not members of the

Federal Reserve System.
Division of Compliance and Consumer Affairs
550 17th Street NW
Washington, D.C. 20429-9990
(202) 736-0000
Web: **http://www.fdic.gov**

- **Federal Reserve System (Fed)**
  Supervises state-chartered banks that are members of the Federal Reserve System.
  Division of Consumer and Community Affairs
  20th St. and Constitution NW
  Federal Reserve Board
  Washington, D.C. 20551
  (202) 452-3693
  Web: **http://www.federalreserve.gov**

- **National Credit Union Administration (NCUA)**
  Charters, supervises, and insures federal credit unions and many state credit unions.
  Compliance Officer
  National Credit Union Administration
  1775 Duke Street
  Alexandria, VA 22314-3428
  (703) 518-6300
  Fraud: (800) 827-9650
  Web: **http://www.ncua.gov**

- **Office of Thrift Supervision (OTS)**
  The primary regulator of all federal, and many state-chartered, thrift institutions, which include savings banks and savings and loans institutions.
  1700 "G" Street NW
  Washington, D.C. 20552

(202) 906-6000
Email: publicinfo@ots.treas.gov
Web: **http://www.ots.treas.gov**

- **U.S. Trustee (UST)**
  Contact the Trustee in the region where fraudulent bankruptcy was filed.
  Web:
  http://www.ots.treas.govhttp://www.usdoj.gov/ust/

- **U.S. Securities and Exchange Commission (SEC)**
  The SEC's Office of Investor Education and Assistance serves investors who complain to the SEC about investment fraud or the mishandling of their investments by securities professionals.
  SEC Office of Investor Education and Assistance
  450 Fifth Street NW
  Washington, D.C. 20549-0213
  (202) 942-7040
  Web: **http://www.ots.treas.govhttp://www.sec.gov/complaint.html**

- **Federal Communications Commission (FCC)**
  For cellular phone and long distance fraud.
  Consumer Information Bureau
  445 12th Street SW, Room 5A863
  Washington, D.C. 20554
  (888) 225-5322
  E-mail: fccinfo@fcc.gov
  Web: **http://www.ots.treas.govhttp://www.fcc.gov**

Privacy Newsletters:

- **Privacy Journal**
  P.O. Box 28577

Providence, RI 02908
(401) 274-7861
Web: **www.privacyjournal.net**
E-mail: orders@privacyjournal.net

- **Privacy Newsletter**
  P.O. Box 8206
  Philadelphia, PA 19101-8206
  E-mail: privacy@mindspring.com

- **Privacy Times**
  P.O. Box 302
  Cabin John, MD 20818
  (301) 229-7002
  Web: **http://www.privacytimes.com**

Privacy Resources and Organizations

Electronic Privacy Information Center. EPIC conducts litigation, sponsors conferences, produces reports, publishes the EPIC Alert, and leads campaigns on privacy issues. For more information email: info@epic.org, or contact EPIC, 1718 Connecticut Avenue, NW, Suite 200, Washington, D. C. 20009. Tel: (202) 483-1140. Executive Director: Marc Rotenberg. **www.epic.org**

Consumers Against Supermarket Privacy Invasion and Numbering. CASPIAN is a national Web-based organization opposing the current trends of supermarkets to require customer information in order to receive discounts. Email kma@nocards.org. Founder: Katherine Albrecht. **www.nocards.org**

Coalition Against Unsolicited Commercial Email. CAUCE is an all-volunteer, entirely Web-based organization, created by Netizens to advocate for a legislative solution to the problem of UCE (spam). CAUCE began as a discussion group called SPAM-LAW, formed of members who felt that legislation was necessary to stop spam from choking the life out of the Internet. Email: comments@cauce.org. President: Edward Cherlin. **www.cauce**

Center for Media Education. A national non-profit organization dedicated to improving the quality of electronic media, especially on the behalf of children and families. Provides guides, reports, and other information on children's and consumer privacy. Contact: cme@cme.org.

Computer Professionals for Social Responsibility. A national membership organization of people concerned about the impact of technology on society. CPSR sponsors working groups on civil liberties, working in the computer industry and others. Contact:

cpsr@cpsr.org or cpsr-info@cpsr.org. PO Box 717, Palo Alto, CA 94302. Tel: (650) 322-3778. Fax: (650) 322-4748. **www.cpsr.org**

Consumer Project on Technology. The CPT is currently focusing on intellectual property rights, healthcare, electronic commerce ad competition policy. Contact: Box 19367, Washington, D. C. 20036, Tel: (202) 387-8030. Fax: (202) 234-5176. Director: James Love.

Electronic Frontier Foundation. Publishes newsletters, Internet Guidebooks and other documents, provides mailing lists and other online forums, and hosts a large electronic document archive. Contact: info@eff.org. 1550 Bryant Street, Ste 725, San Francisco, CA 94103-4832. Tel: (415) 436-9333.
Fax: (415) 436-9993. E-mail: ask@eff.org

Privacy Coalition. A nonpartisan coalition of consumer, civil liberties, educational, family, library, labor, and technology organizations in support of legislation that effectively protects personal privacy. Contact: coalition@privacy.org.

ID Theft Affidavit

Victim Information

(1) My full legal name is

____

(First) (Middle) (Last) (Jr., Sr., III)

(2) (If different from above) When the events described in this affidavit took place, I was known as

____

(First) (Middle) (Last) (Jr., Sr., III)

(3) My date of birth is ______________________
(day / month / year)

(4) My Social Security number is ______________________

(5) My driver's license or identification card state and number are ______________________

(6) My current address is

____

____

City ______________________ State ____________

Zip Code ____________

(7) I have lived at this address since ______________________
(month / year)

(8) (If different from above) When the events described in this affidavit took place, my address was

____

City ________________________ State __________

Zip Code ________________________

(9) I lived at the address in Item 8 from ________ (month/year) until ________ (month/year)

(10) My daytime telephone number is (____) ________________

My evening telephone number is (____) ________________

How the Fraud Occurred

Check all that apply for items 11–17:

(11) ❑ I did not authorize anyone to use my name or personal information to seek the money, credit, loans, goods or services described in this report.

(12) ❑ I did not receive any benefit, money, goods or services as a result of the events described in this report.

(13) ❑ My identification documents (for example, credit cards, birth certificate, driver's license, Social Security card, etc.) were ❑ stolen ❑ lost on or about ________________ (day/month/year).

(14) ❑ To the best of my knowledge and belief, the following person(s) used my information (for example, my name, address, date of birth, existing account numbers, Social Security number, mother's maiden name, etc.) or identification documents to

get money, credit, loans, goods or services without my knowledge or authorization:

____

Name (if known)

____

Address (if known)

____

Phone number(s) (if known)

____

Additional information (if known)

(15) ❑ I do NOT know who used my information or identification documents to get money, credit, loans, goods or services without my knowledge or authorization.

(16) ❑ Additional comments: (For example, description of the fraud, which documents or information were used or how the identity thief gained access to your information.)

____

____

____

(Attach additional pages as necessary.)

Victim's Law Enforcement Actions

(17) (check one) I ❑ am ❑ am not willing to assist in the prosecution of the person(s) who committed this fraud.

(18) (check one) I ❑ am ❑ am not authorizing the release of this information to law enforcement for the purpose of assisting them in the investigation and prosecution of the person(s) who committed this fraud.

(19) (check all that apply) I ❑ have ❑ have not reported the events described in this affidavit to the police or other law enforcement agency. The police ❑ did ❑ did not write a report. In the event you have contacted the police or other law enforcement agency, please complete the following:

____

(Agency #1)

____

(Officer / Agency personnel taking report)

____________________ ____________________

(Date of report) (Report number, if any)

____________________ ____________________

(Phone number) (email address, if any)

____

(Agency #2)

____

(Officer / Agency personnel taking report)

____________________ ____________________

(Date of report) (Report number, if any)

____________________ ____________________

(Phone number) (email address, if any)

Documentation Checklist

Please indicate the supporting documentation you are able to provide to the companies you plan to notify. Attach copies (NOT originals) to the affidavit before sending it to the companies.

(20) ❑ A copy of a valid government-issued photo-identification card (for example, your driver's license, state-issued ID card or your passport). If you are under 16 and don't have a photo-ID, you may submit a copy of your birth certificate or a copy of your official school records showing your enrollment and place of residence.

(21) ❑ Proof of residency during the time the disputed bill occurred, the loan was made or the other event took place (for example, a rental/lease agreement in your name, a copy of a utility bill or a copy of an insurance bill).

(22) ❑ A copy of the report you filed with the police or sheriff's department. If you are unable to obtain a report or report number from the police, please indicate that in Item 19. Some companies only need the report number, not a copy of the report. You may want to check with each company.

(continued on next page)

Signature

I declare under penalty of perjury that the information I have provided in this affidavit is true and correct to the best of my knowledge.

____

(signature)

____

(date signed)

Knowingly submitting false information on this form could subject you to criminal prosecution for perjury.

____

(Notary) [Check with each company. Creditors sometimes require notarization. If they do not, please have one witness (non-relative) sign below that you completed and signed this affidavit.]

Witness:

____

(signature)

____

(printed name)

____________________	____________________
(date)	(telephone number)

Fraudulent Account Statement

Completing this Statement

- Make as many copies of this page as you need. Complete a separate page for each company you're notifying and only send it to that company. Include a copy of your signed affidavit.
- List only the account(s) you're disputing with the company receiving this form. See the example below.
- If a collection agency sent you a statement, letter or notice about the fraudulent account, attach a copy of that document (NOT the original).

I declare (check all that apply):

❑ As a result of the event(s) described in the ID Theft Affidavit, the following account(s) was / were opened at your company in my name without my knowledge, permission or authorization using my personal information or identifying documents:

See chart next page ☞

❑ During the time of the accounts described above, I had the following account open with your company:

Billing name: ______________________________

Billing address: ______________________________

Account number: ______________________________

Creditor Name/Address (the company that opened the account or provided the goods or services)	Account Number	Type of unauthorized credit/goo ds/services provided by creditor	Date issued or opened (if known)	Amount/Value Provided (the amount charged or the cost of the goods/services)
Example Example National Bank 22 Main Street Columbus, Ohio 22722	01234567-89	auto loan	01/05/2002	$25,500.00

Glossary

Ad blocker—software used on your personal computer to prevent advertisements from popping up when you are surfing on the internet. An Ad blocker helps pages load faster and prevents ads from tracking what you're doing while on the internet.

Affirmative consent / Opt-in—you agree to receive certain types of communications or marketing.

Anonymizer—a service on the internet that enables you to surf anonymously and it prevents a website from seeing your e-mail or IP address, or planting cookies on your computer.

Biometric identifier—a personal identifier that distinguishes a human by measuring a physical feature, or a repeatable action. (For example, your hand geometry, retinal scan, iris scan, finger prints, facial characteristics, DNA, voice prints.)

Browser—a software application that enables you to read web pages on the internet.

Cookies—small text files stored on your computer and later retrieved by a web server. They allow the server to keep track of your activities on the internet and connect individual web requests into something like a session. Cookies can also prevent users from having to be authorized for every password protected page. They are usually stored on your PC's hard disk. Cryptic cookies with an unclear purpose which are put in your computer without your knowledge may violate your privacy.

Digital signature–a process used to verify to the person receiving the information through an electronic transmission that the person sending the information is who he or she says they are and that the message has not been changed from the time that it has been transmitted.

Dumpster Diver–refers to a person who sifts through trash for the purpose of gaining information. This is a practice used by identity thieves to gain personal and financial information.

Encryption software–this software scrambles the words that you type so that it is unreadable to people who can intercept your communications. They can't read the document unless there is unscrambling information given to them.

Encryption–the process by which mathematical algorithms convert data into an unreadable format in order to enable secure transmission or storage.

Federal Trade Commission (FTC)–The governmental agency that enforces federal antitrust and consumer protection laws. This commission works to enhance the United States marketplace, and tries to eliminate acts or practices that are unfair or deceptive.

Firewall–a hardware or software device to control access to a computer on a local area network from outside computers on the internet.

Hacking–exploring and manipulating the workings of a computer or other technological device or system, either for the purpose of understanding how it works or to gain unauthorized access.

Identity theft–the use of your personal identifying information in order to fraudulently appropriate an identity for an illegal purpose.

IP address—this address is a unique string of numbers that identifies your computer on the internet or on a network.

Key-loggers—software programs that can report the exact key strokes or exactly what you type on a keyboard. All of your account numbers, passwords, etc are accessible in a log to the person who installed either the software or the external hardware.

Opt-out—You give notice to a particular company or agency that you do not want disclosure of the data that they have the right to disclose unless you object.

Peer To Peer File Sharing—In a peer-to-peer network, computers send messages and requests directly to one another without a server intermediary. Files are shared, including music, Word files, etc.

Phishing—is the use of 'spoofed' e-mails and fraudulent websites designed to fool recipients into divulging personal financial data such as credit card and account numbers, usernames and passwords, social security numbers, etc. By hijacking the trusted brands of well-known banks, online retailers and credit card companies, phishers are able to convince recipients to hand over sensitive information.

Pretexting—use of false pretense including fraudulent calls or e-mails pretending to be a particular entity in order to obtain your personal information such as your Social Security Number, bank account numbers, etc.

Privacy statement—an organization's communication which may be in their handbook or on their web site which alerts others to what personal information is being collected, how it will be used, who it will be shared with, and whether one has the option to exercise how that information will be used.

Profile information–information that is collected about you that is bought, shared, and sold, that associates your information with you. It may give your address, job, financial information, or even the car that you drive.

Redact–means to edit out, erase, black out or hide certain confidential information like all but the last five numbers of your social security number.

Secure Sockets Layer (SSL)–a protocol (set of formal rules that describe how to transmit this data) designed to provide encrypted communication on the internet. You look for the picture of a lock at the bottom of your computer screen that tells you that the information will be encrypted.

Shoulder Surfer–refers to a person who looks over your shoulder or peers at you from afar in order to gain access to your personal information, i.e.; person watching you to acquire your PIN at the ATM machine.

Skimmer–is a small device which captures the information imbedded in the metal strip on your credit card.

Spam–a colloquial term that refers to unsolicited or unwanted e-mail.

Spyware–a program that reports your computer or internet habits and other information to companies or others. It is embedded in other programs that you download without your knowledge.

Index

About The Author

Mari Frank, an attorney, professional trainer, and privacy consultant in private practice in Laguna Niguel, California, has worked in the district attorney's office, practiced law in insurance defense, and has had a general civil law practice. As a mediator, she has successfully resolved thousands of disputes. Ms. Frank is a certified trainer for the State Bar of California, has been a law professor, and currently teaches courses at the University of California. She received her bachelor's degree from the University of Wisconsin (Madison), her master's degree from Hofstra University, and her law degree from Western State University College of Law. She received her post law school negotiation and mediation training from McGeorge School of Law, and Harvard Law School.

As a privacy expert, Ms. Frank has written and compiled *The Identity Theft Survival Kit; From Victim to Victor: A Step By Step Guide To Ending The Nightmare of Identity Theft* (First and Second Edition) and has co-authored *Privacy Piracy* with Beth Givens, the director of the Privacy Rights Clearinghouse. Ms. Frank's own identity was stolen by an impostor who took thousands of dollars, and even assumed her profession as a lawyer. But she refused to be defeated as a victim; instead she chose to help thousands of victims with her web site, books, legislative work, and advocacy.

She has appeared on *Dateline, 48 Hours*, NBC, and ABC *Nightly News, Investigative Reports, The O'Reilly Factor, Connie Chung Tonight,* dozens of other national television programs, and almost 200 radio shows. She has been featured in the *New York Times, The Los Angeles Times, U.S. News and World Report, Money Magazine, The Wall Street Journal, The Washington Post, The Chicago Tribune, The American Bar Journal,* and many other national publications.

Ms. Frank testified several times before the U.S. Senate, the California Legislature, the Federal Trade Commission, the Social Security Administration, and she gave a speech at the White House with former President Bill Clinton in 1999 that was televised on C-Span. She is a sheriff reserve on the High Tech Crime Unit, in Orange County, California. She serves on the advisory board of the State of California Office of Privacy Protection, the Identity Theft Resource Center, and she is a consultant for the governmental Office of Victims of Crimes. Ms. Frank provides testimony, consulting, and training programs on privacy and identity theft to law enforcement, governmental agencies, and national corporations.

Ms. Frank recently hosted and presented a live seminar for PBS Television entitled "Identity Theft: Protecting Yourself in the Information Age." This nationally aired program included a pledge drive for public television. Two of her books, *Safeguard Your Identity: Protect Yourself With a Personal Privacy Audit,* and *From Victim To Victor: A Step-By-Step Guide For Ending the Nightmare of Identity Theft,* Second Edition with CD, and the video of her live presentation, served as pledge gifts when the viewing audience made donations to support Public Television.

For more information about privacy and identity theft, Ms. Frank's background, services and other publications, please visit **www.identitytheft.org** and **www.MariFrank.com**. You may also contact her at:

Mari J. Frank, Esq. and Associates
28202 Cabot Road, Suite 300
Laguna Niguel, California 92677
949-364-1511
949-363-7561 - fax

To order books from Porpoise Press, Inc;
Call 800-725-0807

Or Visit Identity Theft Prevention and Survival
at **www.identitytheft.org**.

LEARN MORE ABOUT PROTECTING YOUR IDENTITY!

From Victim to Victor: A Step-By-Step Guide for Ending the Nightmare of Identity Theft, 2nd Edition (With CD)
Mari Frank, Esq.
232 pages • 8.5 × 11 • $39.95

This book and CD bring hope and real results to the victims of identity theft who have had nowhere to turn for help until now. The materials provide crucial information showing you the actions and precautions you need to take to minimize your risk of identity theft. And, if you become a victim, this book coaches you through every action you must take, who you must contact, what you need to say, how to complete the pre-formatted letters and essential forms, and how to regain your most valuable asset-your identity. It is a lifesaver.

This book will empower you with:

- Easy-to-follow steps to protect your identity and regain it if stolen
- Easily understood legal explanations of your rights
- Attorney-composed, pre-formatted letters (on CD) to write, to protect your rights without having to hire a lawyer
- Successful techniques to handle every issue to protect your privacy and good name

---

From Victim to Victor CD
Mari Frank, Esq.
$29.95 • CD (for PC or Mac)
Complete with attorney-composed fill-in-the-blank letters, forms, logs and resources

This CD contains letters, forms, logs, an affidavit, and resources, allowing you to complete essential correspondence to various agencies by filling in the blanks, completing the forms and affidavit, and surfing directly to dozens of helpful website resources. You'll have peace of mind knowing you have written a professional legal letter to solve your problems. It's like having your own lawyer coaching you at a fraction of the cost of even one hour of attorney time. You'll save hundreds of hours and thousands of dollars of attorney fees.

Identity Theft: Protecting Yourself in the Information Age DVD
As seen on PBS Television
Mari Frank, Host
Santa Fe Productions, 2004
$29.95

This one-hour seminar hosted by Mari Frank shows the hundreds of ways we are vulnerable to invasion of privacy and identity theft. This program shows how you are at risk and gives you a strategy to protect yourself and reduce your chances of becoming a victim. **(Available July 1, 2005)**

IDENTITY THEFT PREVENTION AND SURVIVAL PRODUCT ORDER FORM

Order Anytime:
Toll Free Telephone Orders: **(800) 725-0807** • Fax Orders: **(949) 363-7561**
Order Online: **www.identitytheft.org**
Mail Orders:
Porpoise Press, Inc. • 28202 Cabot Road, Suite 300 • Laguna Niguel, CA 92677

Ordered by:
Name: ____________________
Address: ____________________
City, State Zip: ____________________
Daytime Telephone: ____________________
E-mail address: ____________________

Ship to:
Name: ____________________
Address: ____________________
City, State, Zip: ____________________
Evening Telephone: ____________________

☐ Check ☐ Money order enclosed $__________
Make payable to: **Porpoise Press, Inc.**
Bill my:
☐ MasterCard / Visa # ______-______-______-______
CCID (Credit Card Identification No., 3 digit # on back of card) ______
Exp. Date: ____/____
Signature: ____________________

Qty	Title	Price	Total
	Safeguard Your Identity: Protect Yourself With a Personal Privacy Audit	$15.95	
	From Victim to Victor: A Step-By-Step Guide for Ending the Nightmare of Identity Theft, 2nd Edition (book with CD)	39.95	
	From Victim to Victor CD only (With steps, letters, forms)	29.95	
	Identity Theft: Protecting Yourself in the Information Age DVD (available 7/01/05)	29.95	

Subtotal = $______
7.75% tax (California residents only) = $______
Shipping & Handling = $______
Total = $______

Shipping and Handling Charges
Orders will be sent Priority Mail unless otherwise specified.
Safeguard Your Identity, From Victim to Victor CD only,
or *Identity Theft* DVD (up to 1 pound) = $4.95
From Victim to Victor, book with CD (up to 2 lbs.) = $6.95
Multiple products based on weight (3 lbs) = $8.95
add $2 per additional pound or portion thereof.
For international or FedEx shipping, please call to get a price quote.

Are you a:
☐Victim of Identity Theft ☐Concerned Consumer
☐Other ____________________

PORPOISE PRESS, INC.

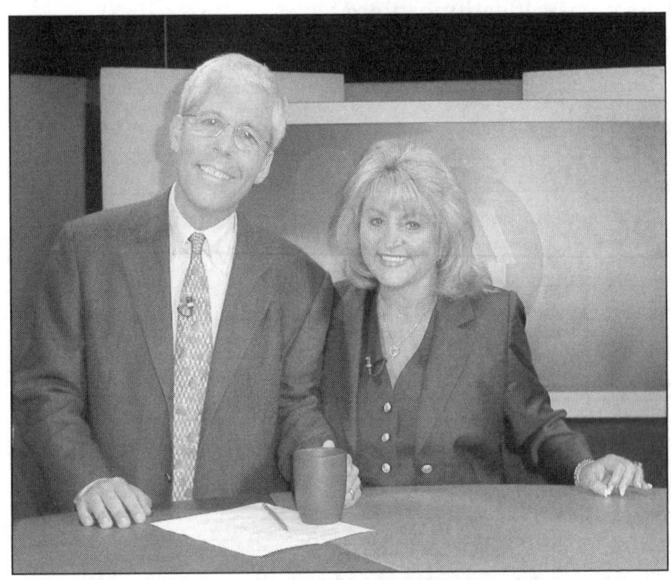

Mari Frank with PBS Television host Greg Sherwood.

I was honored to present the 90-minute television special by Santa Fe Productions, *Identity Theft: Protecting Yourself in the Information Age*. In this interactive seminar with a live audience, I provided identity theft and privacy protection education to the viewing audience across the nation. To help promote other educational seminars sponsored by Public Television, I participated in the pledge portion of the show. During these segments, I was interviewed by the lively host, Greg Sherwood. It was a privilege to have my books and the video of the show offered as gifts to the home viewers when they called in donations to support Public Television.

I extend my gratitude to Santa Fe Productions and PBS Television for their desire to inform America about privacy and identity fraud concerns. I send a very special thank you and my very best wishes to *you*, my readers, for your willingness to protect yourself, your family, and your country from this epidemic. In this information age, be assured, you must Safeguard Your Identity and Protect Yourself with a Personal Privacy Audit.

Thank you,
Mari J. Frank